ESCAPE FROM CLUELESSNESS

ESCAPE FROM CLUELESSNESS

A Guide for the Organizationally Challenged

Lee G. Bolman and
Terrence E. Deal

AMACOM
American Management Association
New York • Atlanta • Boston • Chicago • Kansas City • San Francisco • Washington, D.C.
Brussels • Mexico City • Tokyo • Toronto

Special discounts on bulk quantities of AMACOM books are available to corporations, professional associations, and other organizations. For details, contact Special Sales Department, AMACOM, a division of American Management Association, 1601 Broadway, New York, NY 10019.
Tel.: 212-903-8316. Fax: 212-903-8083.
Web site:www.amanet.org

Library of Congress Cataloging-in-Publication Data

Bolman, Lee G.
Escape from cluelessness: a guide for the organizationally challenged: an antidote to cynicism, confusion, corporate doublespeak, and other ailments of today's workplace / Lee G. Bolman and Terrence E. Deal.
p. cm.
Includes bibliographical references and index.
ISBN 0-8144-7071-8
1. Office politics. 2. Organizational change. 3. Work environment.
I. Title: Guide for the organizationally challenged. II. Deal, Terrence E. III. Title.
HF5386.5.B65 2000
650.1'3—dc21 *00–020156*

Printed in the United States of America.

Printing number

10 9 8 7 6 5 4 3 2 1

Contents

Acknowledgments

Although you might suspect that writing about clueless-ness would come pretty easily to Bolman and Deal, the truth is, we couldn't have done this book without a lot of help from many friends and colleagues. We got many ideas and insights from audiences at the 1998 and 1999 Organizational Behavior Teaching Conferences, at the 1998 International Conference on Business and Consciousness, and at the 1999 meeting of the Academy of Management.

Among the many individuals who provided helpful reactions and feedback are Ella Bell, David Bradford, Ellen Castro, Robina Chatham, Jim Clawson, Robin Johnson, Kathy Kane, Robert Kramer, Mark Mallinger, Bob Marx, Marilyn Taylor, and Peter Vail. At UMKC, Bill Eddy, just retired as Dean of the Bloch School of Business and Public Administration, and Nancy Day, director of the Business Administration Division, provided a supportive environment that helped Lee stay sane and at least marginally productive. Gib Henschke, Dean of the Rossier School at the University of Southern California, and Associate Dean Estela Beasimon paved the way for Terry's successful transition from Vanderbilt back to California. Students in two of Lee's leadership courses at the Bloch School also provided many helpful reactions. Syl Higgins and Mary Yung both contributed vital operational support. In Nashville, Homa Aminmadani continued to bring remarkable levels of order and support to Terry.

Our longtime friend and editor, Bill Hicks, came through for us once again with enormously helpful guidance and support. We'll always remember this as the project in which both Bill's and Lee's mothers died within a few months of each other in the late stages of writing. (Thankfully, Terry's parents continue to be models of energy and durability.) The book had to move to the back burner for a while, but our collective capacity to make it through some very challenging times confirmed the depth of our friendship and support for one another.

As always, Lee is grateful to his children, Edward, Shelley, Lori, Scott, Christopher, and Bradley. They taught him much of what he knows about organizations, leadership, and the challenge of escaping from cluelessness. Terry's daughter, Janie, continues to be a font of love, encouragement, and critique.

We've thanked our wives, Sandy Deal and Joan Gallos, in every book we've written together. They deserve it more every time. We're humbled, grateful, even pleasantly surprised that, as we enter a new millennium, Joan and Sandy are both still with us. Their love, support, and deep friendship keep us going.

ESCAPE FROM CLUELESSNESS

INTRODUCTION

This book is about escaping a debilitating modern affliction—cluelessness at work. To find out if you, or those around you, are among the clueless, try the following quiz, designed by two fully trained social scientists (who make no claim for its validity or reliability). If you answer yes to at least six of these questions, keep reading.

- Do you work in anything larger than a sidewalk fruit stand? (The bigger the workplace, the better the chance of chronic confusion.)
- Have you ever wondered why so many people in high positions seem to be selfish, power-crazed boneheads? (Usually, they're not boneheads, just clueless. Chapter 1 explains why.)
- Does your workplace often seem chaotic and weirdly unpredictable? Have you ever wished for help in clearing up the confusion? (Your place is probably no weirder than most. Read Chapter 2 for six ways to cut through the craziness.)
- Do you detest office politics? (Office politics are here to stay, but Chapter 3 shows you how to get through the minefield.)
- Do you ever feel like a doormat, powerless to affect things that really matter? (Chapter 4 explains the ins

and outs of political games and shows how you can increase your clout.)

- Do relationships at work remind you of a dysfunctional family? (If so, the lessons in Chapter 5 can help you know yourself and achieve better relationships with others.)
- Does your employer seem to embrace the philosophy that the beatings will continue until morale improves? Do managers treat everyone like dirt and still expect them to give their best? (Chapter 6 gives you the scoop on how to improve your workplace, or find a better one.)
- Does your company sometimes feel like a feudal manor straight out of the Middle Ages? (It probably is. Every human group has a pecking order. Chapter 7 explains why—and what to do about it.)
- Would the motto "Confusion R Us" be a perfect slogan for your workplace? Do you ever wonder what the goals are or try to figure out why people work at cross-purposes? (Chapter 8 provides guidelines for squeezing in a few more productive moments.)
- Have you ever felt like an outsider at work, struggling to decipher mysterious local traditions and folkways? Do you ever feel as though you're in a weird contest where everyone plays by different rules? (Chapter 9 explains how to read workplace culture and understand what's really going on below the surface.)
- Does your workplace feel glueless as well as clueless? Do you work for the only bosses who haven't yet discovered the benefits of a cohesive culture? (Chapter 10 outlines some strategies for overcoming toxic or sterile work environments.)
- Does your workplace bumble through one failed

change effort after another? Is leadership notable mostly for its absence? Do bosses seem to have copied the leadership style of Attila the Hun? (Chapter 11 explains how to cope with change and lead from where you are.)
- Do you sometimes worry that your career and your life are going in the wrong direction? Or that they're going nowhere? (Chapter 12 describes four different life paths. Plot a course that's right for you.)
- Do you wish you could quit, but you're either too young or too poor to retire? (Don't bail out yet! You probably have more options than you realize. We'll point out some promising possibilities.)

Escape from Cluelessness is both an atlas and a guidebook. When you're planning a trip, an atlas maps the terrain to help you think ahead and avoid getting lost. We've tried to build a Rand McNally's of the workplace to help you get your bearings in a strange and puzzling territory. A good atlas does two things. It maps the big picture, and it offers more detailed charts for local highways and byways. The "Escape Map" at the beginning of Part I shows the big picture—the major stops on the journey from cluelessness to a better life at work.

First, we focus on system dynamics, the basic code you have to know to make sense of any workplace. From there, our tour plunges into the murky underworld of politics. You'll learn how to map political minefields and get enough power to get things done. The next stop is the emotional world of people at work. You'll find ways to improve relationships with others and to make a bad job better. Then it's on to the red-tape land of bureaucracy. You'll study feudalism—a guided tour of monarchs and serfs. You'll learn some tricks for shaping structure to work for you for instead of creating bureaucratic barriers. From there, plunge into the depths of tribal life at work. Learn how to decode cultural puzzles. Even better, pick up some ways to give the workplace a little more excitement, fun, and pizzazz. Near journey's end, we take a fresh look at change and leadership. You'll learn ways to survive the endless changes that keep sweeping over you, and how to nudge things in more positive directions. Finally, we examine a deeper question that's a silent companion at work: What life path do you really want to follow?

A good guidebook offers more than maps. It also identifies sights and places you really need to know about. It reveals secrets known only to insiders. It tells you how to get from one place to another. That's what we've tried to do in this book. You be the judge of how well we've done.

FRANK 'N' HOPE: *WELCOME TO ALCATRAZ*

Frank: You're new here?

Hope: Second day on the job.

Frank: Welcome to Alcatraz!

Hope: You don't like it here?

Frank: Maybe it's a little better than a dip in an acid bath.

Hope: So why stay?

Frank: Last place I worked was worse. A 9-to-5 strait-jacket. But here the boss is so dumb he's gotta be depriving a village somewhere of an idiot.

Hope: The best thing about your job is a clueless boss?

Frank: Except for lunch and coffee breaks.

Hope: I'm hoping for something better.

Frank: Newcomers' syndrome. Couple of weeks, you'll be over it.

Welcome to Alcatraz introduces you to a pair of co-workers named Frank and Hope. You'll run into them again from time to time. They're our odd couple serving as a workplace Greek chorus. Frank and Hope work in the same office, but have little in common. Hope is an optimistic, idealistic newcomer. She really believes that a workplace can offer buoyancy and zest. Frank? Well, he could captain a bowling team called the Seasoned Cynics. They're caricatures—exaggerated examples of very different reactions to life at the office. Depending on your view of life and work, you might see Frank as realistic and Hope as naive. Or, Hope constructive and Frank corrosively cynical. Either way, we hope you'll enjoy their dialogues and find that they help clarify your own thinking. As you can see from the preceding conversation, their relationship got off to a rocky start the first time they met.

DOES WORK SUCK?

Frank and Hope represent two sides of a long-running debate about the place of work in our lives. Hope looks at the bright side: She thinks work can and should be productive, rewarding, and fun. As far as Frank is concerned, work sucks. Always has and always will. It's an inescapable prison with a paycheck that funds life outside the workweek. There are lots of Franks and Hopes around, although they answer to different names in your office. You may identify more with one than the other. Each may speak for different sides of an ongoing tug-of-war in your own feelings about work. The Frank 'n' Hope debate seeps into lots of offices, factory floors, truck stops, taverns, and homes. Their contrasting views even show up in books and newspapers. As one example, consider the following dialogue between leadership expert Warren Bennis and canine consultant Dogbert (an alter ego for cartoonist Scott Adams) in the *Los Angeles Times*. There was no official scorekeeper, so judge for yourself the outcome of this jaw-to-paw face-off between wise man and malevolent cartoon canine:

Question: What are the biggest issues facing managers as we approach the 21st century?

BENNIS: The most obvious is the incredible change going on in terms of technology and globalization. This affects all modern organizations today and has created great confusion. . . . Another big issue is the shareholder-versus-stakeholder debate. Are corporations responsible to shareholders or to the community, the workers, and suppliers? . . . Then there's trust, or what I call the Dilbert factor. Unfortunately, Dilbert has such resonance because of the deep and dangerous cynicism out there in the workplace. And I think that's sad.

DOGBERT: The biggest challenge will be brainwashing the gullible employees into thinking there's a good reason to work long hours of uncompensated overtime. I recommend calling this process "coaching" so they won't realize it's a bad thing.*

Bennis is an elegant writer and one of the world's foremost experts on leadership and organizational behavior. We're among his biggest fans. But he was hard-pressed by a canine cartoon creation of Scott Adams, the 1990s' improbable management guru. When we've asked audiences to judge the results of this jaw-to-paw debate, the vote has been closely divided. Some favor Adams, some Bennis, and others call it a draw.

Inspired by his years as a "necktie-wearing, corporate victim assigned to cubicle 4S700R at the headquarters of Pacific Bell," Adams created Dilbert, a corporate everyman who wanders mindlessly through a monotonous landscape of confining cubicles, clueless workers, incompetent bosses, bureaucratic inertia, and corporate doublespeak. His irreverent daily send-up of bosses and corporations has earned him millions of fans. Dilbert and company can be found taped to

*From Denise Hamilton, "Dog vs. Man: Two High-Powered Management Experts Go Paw to Hand Over Workplace Issues," *Los Angeles Times*, February 24, 1997.

walls and bulletin boards of companies all over North America and beyond.

CAN YOU MAKE WORK BETTER?

Scott Adams has successfully tapped a huge reservoir of workplace frustration and cynicism. He brilliantly skewers foibles and hypocrisy we've all experienced from time to time. But he stops short of addressing some big questions: How do we become smarter about organizations? What do we do when it's too painful to laugh? Most important of all, what can we do to escape cubicle confinement?

One reason Adams doesn't address such questions is that he doubts you can do much. His advice is do what he did—quit and go to work for yourself—because it's a waste of time trying to improve whatever is wrong with your situation. A lot of workers feel the same way. They believe that you put up with boring jobs, tyrannical bosses, impossible demands, silly rules, and lousy pay because that's the best you can do. You hold your nose, lay low, and grab the paycheck.

Perversely, it's comforting and reassuring to believe you can't do anything. It means you're not responsible. You don't have to think about options. You feel no obligation to do anything new or different. But such comfort creates a hidden self-made trap. You blame your inertia on others—the boss, the company, the capitalist system, or whatever. But it's a mistake to assume that there's nothing that you can do.

You do have options. John Dewey once said that freedom rests on the power to choose between known alternatives. This book is a guide, even a goad, to expand your possibilities and to free yourself from a mind- and spirit-numbing daily grind. We point out options you may not have seen before. We run down realistic strategies for workplace improvement. We show you how to take reasonable risks without betting or buying the farm. We show you how to get some help from your friends, and steer you away from really dumb moves and suicide missions.

Read Dilbert and you learn that organizations are screwed up because the people who run them are clueless, selfish, and hypocritical. It's a popular message with more than a grain of truth. We've all had our share of bad bosses. But it's not the whole story. This book fills a gap between satirical cynicism and the rosy, one-big-happy-and-efficient family stuff that management often touts. We explain why your workplace might feel just like Dilbert's. But we also offer practical ideas for making things better. Somewhere between corrosive cynicism and romantic fluff is a middle ground of realistic optimism. It's not easy ground to find. This book is a guide.

PART I

IS THERE A CURE FOR CLUELESSNESS?

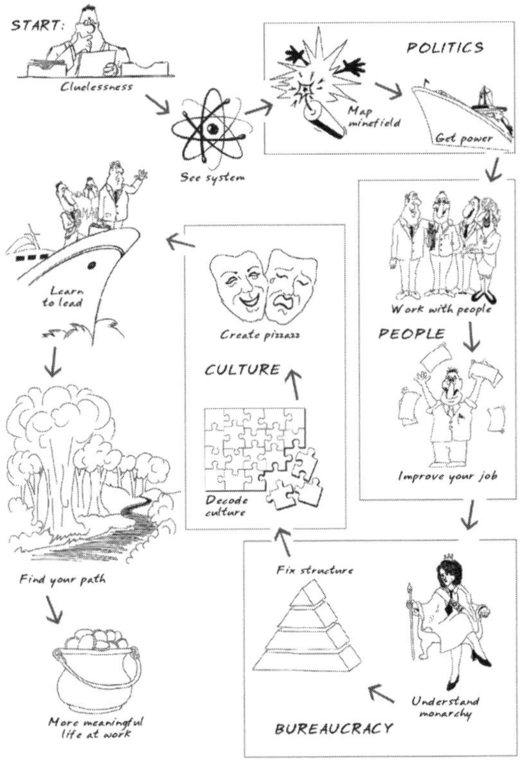

Escape Map

1

Clues for the Clueless: Making Sense of Work

You're not alone if work often seems crazy. A lot of people ponder the same questions. Why do so many managers emphasize appearances and politics over productivity? Why do organizations squander motivation and loyalty by treating employees like garbage? Why do companies keep jumping on new management fads even though the last ones bombed? Why are there so many silly rules and procedures that constantly undermine productivity? Why do so many managers say one thing while doing the opposite? Did they all learn the ropes at hypocrisy school? This book provides some answers that help you make more sense of your job and your workplace.

Bosses from hell abound in movies and comic strips. In film, sometimes they're arrogant, evil men (like Jon Voight's swaggering villain in *Enemy of the State*, Gordon Gekko in *Wall Street*, or the male chauvinist pig played by Dabney Coleman in *Nine to Five*). Other times, they're scheming shrews (like Sigourney Weaver as a cynical self-promoter in *Working Girl*, or the unforgettable classic of the genre, Nurse Ratched in *One Flew Over the Cuckoo's Nest*). *Disclosure*, an equal-opportunity film, offered bad bosses of both genders: Donald Sutherland as a slick and slimy chief executive officer (CEO), along with Demi Moore as a viciously manipulative fast-tracker. Narrow-minded, bureaucratic administrators are automatic features of any movie set in schools (*Mr. Holland's Opus, Dangerous Minds, The Breakfast Club,* and many more). In the daily comics, you find a series of bumbling tyrants: Mr. Dithers in *Dagwood,* Sarge in *Beetle Bailey,* the king in *Wizard of ID*. The ultimate 1990s example is Dilbert's pointy-haired boss. Old pointy-hair is so technically challenged that he can't tell a laptop computer from an Etch-a-Sketch (see Figure 1-1). When he heard that the company needed more Unix programmers, he thought they wanted eunuchs. The misunderstanding almost produced an eerie new surgical benefit for the male staff. Are bosses really that dumb? It must seem that way to a lot of Dilbert fans. And to the growing number of disenchanted employees who are erecting websites to vent their many complaints about work in general or their company in partic-

Figure 1-1. Are bosses clueless?

ular. Daniel Levine's *Disgruntled* site* features an online magazine devoted to stories of dumb bosses and workplace folly. You could probably contribute a few tales of your own.

Dilbert draws millions of readers daily into a workplace that is both bizarre and familiar. Everyone is clueless, cynical, or both. No one knows the goals. Decisions are rarely made, and productive work is as likely as snow in Honolulu. Employees spend most of their time avoiding work, criticizing their bosses, or producing useless garbage in response to mindless directives. Customers are ignored. Bosses and subordinates are at war. Same for engineers and marketers. The human resource department is hostile to people, and everyone hates the accountants. Yet Dilbert's loyal readers often say that they like the strip because it *tells the truth*!

There's a certain smug satisfaction in believing that everyone is clueless but me and thee. It's easy to criticize your parents until you have kids. It's equally convenient to bash bosses until you get promoted. If you want work to mean something but your job is relentlessly tedious, it feels good to blame *someone*—almost any handy target will do. In a perfect world, work would be reasonably sensible and orderly: Go to work, do your duty, and go home. Even such minimal expectations are rarely met. Coworkers arrive with their unique charms and foibles. Some days it's tough to string together a few lucid moments in an office dominated by mood swings, bodily yearnings, emotional conflicts, and personal quirks. Bosses are universal scapegoats, but we all deserve some of the blame. We know things are fouled up, but we're usually clueless about how to make them better.

*Websites are often here today and gone tomorrow, but at the time of writing, you could find Levine's e-zine, and links to many other work-related sites, at http://www.disgruntled.com.

Deep down, we yearn for something better that seems just out of reach.

We're organizationally handicapped because modern workplaces are too complicated for us to understand them. Think of the worst subject you ever encountered at school—the tough slog that made you feel like a terminal dolt: Ms. Hardy's high-attrition algebra course, or Professor Wittgenstein's impenetrable rendition of organic chemistry. Work is often like that. You arrive at the office and blow a few pop quizzes before the morning coffee break. Generally no one notices your lapses because everyone's groping around in the same fog. Year after year some of the best and brightest managers maneuver or meander their way to the top of great enterprises. Then they manage to do really dumb things. Like the loyal son who made sure his dad would live in history by naming a car after him. It was called the Edsel. Or the General Motors boss who persuaded his unions to take a pay cut and then announced big bonuses for top executives. Or the guys at IBM who couldn't see how a tiny company run by a boyish geek named Bill Gates would ever be much of a threat.

How do bright people manage to be so dim? One theory is that they're too bright for their own good. Mortimer Feinberg and John Tarrant, in their book *Why Smart People Do Dumb Things* (New York: Simon & Schuster, 1995), gave it a fancy name—the Self-Destructive Intelligence Syndrome. Feinberg, a psychologist, thinks smart people act stupid because of personality flaws—things like pride, arrogance, and unconscious needs to fail. In their book *When Smart People Work for Dumb Bosses* (New York: McGraw-Hill, 1998), William and Kathleen Lundin came to a similar conclusion: "[Bosses'] dumb behavior is motivated by self-love and ego, which block the capacity for empathy." Psychic flaws have been plain enough in brilliantly self-destructive people like Adolf Hitler, Richard Nixon, and, as you probably noticed, Bill Clinton. But on the whole, the intellectually challenged have at least as many psychological problems as the best and brightest. The real source of cluelessness is not personality or I.Q. It's in *how we think and how we make sense of the world around us*. Regardless of intellectual wattage, we're all out to lunch if we use the wrong ideas for the situation at hand. It's like trying to find your way around San Francisco with a map of New York. Both cities have roads, tall buildings, and water, but that won't keep you from getting hopelessly lost. When we see a distorted picture, we do the wrong thing. But we'll probably stick with our map if it's the only one we've got. So our blinders mask our mistakes. We insist that everything is humming along. Or, if it's not, at least it's not our fault.

FRANK 'N' HOPE: *WORKING WITH DOLTS*

Frank:	It's not my fault if I work with dolts.
Hope:	You included?
Frank:	Rarely. But I'm always looking for some smart company. Maybe you're not as dumb as you look.

Confusion mushrooms as the world keeps becoming more complicated. Lots of bright, well-meaning people keep producing improvements—programmable VCRs, new computer software, multinational corporations, roaming charges, leveraged buyouts, telemarketing, and new tax laws—to name only a few. But progress only seems to plunge us deeper into a dense fog. As Scott Adams puts it in *The Dilbert*

Principle (New York: HarperBusiness, 1996, p. 9): "All the technology that surrounds us, all the management theories, the economic models that predict and guide our behavior, the science that helps us live to eighty—it's all created by a tiny percentage of deviant smart people. The rest of us are treading water as fast as we can. The world is too complex for us. Evolution didn't keep up. We got knowledge and technology before we got intelligence. We're a planet of nearly six billion ninnies living in a civilization that was designed by a few thousand amazingly smart deviants."

The deviant smart folks have created a world that floods us with information. We often feel we're drinking from a fire hydrant. A nonstop stream comes at us via television, newspapers, cell phones, fax, E-mail, the Internet, and just about every other form of communication except maybe smoke signals. It's almost impossible to make much sense of it all and even tougher to figure out how to act on the information we have. Lots of folks are eager to help, often at a hefty price. An army of experts—consultants, politicians, journalists, academics, even the authors of this book—pours out a torrent of ideas, answers, and solutions. No one can keep up, and it's tough to sort the garbage from the good stuff. As we become more informed, we get more confused. To escape bewilderment, we grab any idea that seems to make things clearer. It could be reengineering, enterprise computing, seven habits, *The Celestine Prophecy*, or the daily horoscope. Whatever. Then we clutch our new insight like a two-year-old hugging a Beanie Baby. We feel better because things appear to make more sense. But our security blanket is a mirage. We've donned a new pair of rose-colored glasses. Things look simpler because the lenses filter out a lot of complicated stuff that used to bug us. Sooner or later we crash into something we didn't see. Like the iceberg that sank the

Titanic. Why worry about icebergs if you know your ship is unsinkable?

Until the inevitable crash, misguided managers think they're very smart. An example: Sewell Avery, CEO of the then-giant retailer Montgomery-Ward, refused to spend money on expansion after World War II. He sat by and watched while his company sat out the world's biggest orgy of consumer spending. In the decade after the war, sales at archrival Sears doubled. Ward's went down 10 percent. Avery was clueless. But not dumb. After all, he'd steered Montgomery-Ward very successfully through the depression of the 1930s. After the war, though, he bet on the wrong guru—a famous economist who thought the economy looked pretty shaky. It made sense to Avery because he'd studied history. He noticed that war often led to depression. Avery had charts in his office going all the way back to Napoleon to prove it. The smart thing, he figured, was to keep Ward's cash safe in the bank while the other fools spent themselves into bankruptcy.* If the Great Depression had repeated itself, he could have made the managers' Hall of Fame. It didn't. He ended up in the Hall of Shame instead.

It's easy to catalogue managerial folly, but rarely does anyone admit to going blindly down the wrong path. One of the very few public examples is Robert McNamara, architect of U.S. strategy in the Vietnam war. Thirty years later, he concluded that he and his White House colleagues were "wrong, terribly wrong." He reluctantly conceded that they didn't really know what was going on in Vietnam, *though they thought they did.* Part of their problem was a subtle information gap—most of the top experts on Vietnam had been

*Robert Sobel provides a detailed account of the Montgomery-Ward story in Chapter 12 of his book, *When Giants Stumble: Classic Business Blunders and How to Avoid Them* (Paramus, NJ: Prentice-Hall, 1999), pp. 239–258.

forced out of government during the McCarthy era. Despite incomplete information, McNamara and fellow policy-makers had embraced a concept that seemed sensible. They remembered Munich, where Neville Chamberlain had tried to secure "peace in our time" by letting Hitler annex a big chunk of Czechoslovakia. Appease "the Reds," their thinking went, and the Communists will take all of Asia—like Hitler's Nazis in Europe. A lot of people died for that flawed vision. Everybody since has been trying to avoid another Vietnam, which in due time may produce another Munich. The signs of the times are usually hard to read and even harder to interpret. It's easy to get confused by false glimmers anchored in old assumptions.

Confusion isn't so damaging if you realize you're not playing with a full deck. Most of us have enough sense not to handle our own legal affairs, diagnose our ills, or fill our own cavities. We usually pay attention to visible signs with clear messages like "DANGER—QUALIFIED TECHNICIANS ONLY—RISK OF INJURY OR VIOLENT AND PAINFUL DEATH!!!" Unfortunately, most workplaces don't post such obvious warnings, and there's rarely a qualified technician on duty. Many self-proclaimed experts are actually as bewildered as the rest of us, but firmly convinced of their own delusions. Sometimes they're more dangerous than the problems they claim to solve, because their self-assured muddling digs us into an even deeper hole. Too bad consultants don't always subscribe to the physician's Hippocratic Oath: Above all else, do no harm.

FRANK 'N' HOPE: *CONSULTANTS*

Frank:	Can you believe what they're paying the consultants they just brought in?
Hope:	Maybe they can help. You always say this place is a dung pit.
Frank:	You haven't seen the endless parade. Tailored suits. Glib talk. Big fees. No help. You know the story about consultants. They borrow your watch, tell you the time, and keep the watch. Stick around. You'll see.
Hope:	Maybe. But when your kids are sick, do you treat them yourself?
Frank:	No need. The insurance covers everything.

So how do we escape the cluelessness trap? For starters, it helps to recognize that it comes in different forms, as summarized in Table 1-1. One is *personal* cluelessness. It comes from not knowing enough about ourselves, our actions, or our impact on other people. The symptoms are blindness and hypocrisy. Our actions are counterproductive because we don't know what we're doing. Others think we're pretending to be something we're not. The escape route is via learning about ourselves and getting better at understanding the people we work with.

A second kind of cluelessness is *situational.* This is what we suffer when our work world is too complicated, and we latch on to ideas that aren't as good as they seem. The only way out is to get smarter. Not by pumping out a few more points on an IQ test (though that couldn't hurt). But instead by upgrading our intellectual toolbox with better ideas to bring focus to a fuzzy world. At work, our ideas fail us in several key areas. We're often baffled by *structure and systems,* which are complicated and getting more so. We're also mystified, and often appalled by ongoing *political games* of power and self-interest. They persist everywhere despite our best efforts to purge them or push them under a rug. If that's not enough, there's the challenge of decoding *culture and symbols,* the subtle but powerful traditions and folkways that play a powerful role in every family, group, and workplace.

Deepest and toughest to deal with is *spiritual* cluelessness. We're spiritually clueless when we're not sure about our beliefs, our values, or the life path we really want to follow. The only remedy is to come to grips with basic questions all of us need to answer: What does our life mean? What values should we live by? What are we here to do? Modern workplaces offer little help in finding answers to these perplexing queries. As a result, too many of us drift along with little sense of direction and without a moral compass to guide us through the ethically slippery world of work. This deepens our discouragement about work and, ultimately, about life. You probably know people who are situationally smart but spiritually bankrupt. Take the aforementioned canine consultant Dogbert. He easily manipulates gullible humans around him, but he's ethically stunted, even downright evil. In one of the more famous Dilbert strips, Dogbert explains a new device for firing employees: the "can-o-matic." Situated in restroom stalls, this technological wonder randomly slaps pink slips on employees' backs and flings them out the window. The boss likes the idea, but wishes he could see the expression on people's faces as they fly out of the building. No problem, says Dogbert. They'll just add a video camera.

The wellsprings of cluelessness won't run dry anytime soon, and we're all vulnerable. If you're hoping for miracles,

Table 1-1. Three forms of cluelessness.

Type	*Symptoms*	*Remedy*
Personal	Hypocrisy, blindness	Learning about self
Situational	Confusion, misguided actions	Developing better ideas, more organizational know-how
Ethical, spiritual	Feeling lost, stuck, or confused about your life	Deepening your spiritual journey

quick-and-easy recipes, or a fast track to stock options and executive jets, check your antenna. You are not getting the right picture. We're not selling quick fixes. We try to offer provocative and productive ideas to help you make more sense of what goes on around you. It will take effort and persistence. If you stay with us, you should discover order, even beauty, you never knew your workplace had. Even better, you'll have more fun and get more done.

ESCAPING CLUELESSNESS I: FACING THE PROBLEM

- WORK IS OFTEN CONFUSING AND CHAOTIC.
- WE NEED TO UNDERSTAND WHY WE'RE CLUELESS AND WHAT WE CAN DO ABOUT IT.
- WE'RE AT RISK OF THREE FORMS OF CLUELESSNESS:
  - WE DON'T KNOW OURSELVES.
  - WE DON'T KNOW WHAT'S GOING ON.
  - WE DON'T KNOW WHERE WE'RE GOING.

2

Seeing Systems: Beyond Blame and Linear Thinking

Life at work makes a lot more sense if you learn some basic ideas about how systems work. Things are easier when you (a) know the right buttons to push, (b) can turn surprises into opportunities, and (c) can anticipate delays between actions and consequences. Remember the first law of holes: when you're in one, stop digging. In short, replace simplistic thinking with systemic thinking.

Common sense is a wonderful thing. It gets us through a lot of life's daily challenges. But to understand our workplaces, we need some uncommon sense that's rarely taught in homes or schools. Consider the following example from *L'Express*:

In 1998, French government auditors turned up some puzzling business practices in the Farm Credit Bureau (Crédit Agricole), a government agency in Corsica. The bureau regularly lent large sums of money to borrowers who gave no evidence of ability to repay. Many clients were repeat customers who had never bothered to make payments on prior loans. Repayment was pretty much voluntary, since the agency didn't dun clients for payments. One didn't even have to be a farmer to get a loan. Borrowers included owners of restaurants, bars, and campgrounds, as well as a woman who was apparently farming in a fashionable neighborhood of Paris. One satisfied customer used his farm loan to buy an unconventional set of agricultural vehicles, including a BMW Series 5, a Fiat, and a Land-Rover. Another borrower must have viewed his mistress as a farm worker, because she benefitted handsomely from his loan. Ultimately, a number of individuals in and out of government were arrested. At last word, the cases were wending their way through the French legal system.*

It happened in France. But similar stories of incompetence and misconduct show up everywhere. Just one more scandal to support a widespread belief that public officials are corrupt. This assumption provides a ready-made, all-purpose explanation when government misfires: Blame the politicians. It's a pretty simple model of how things work:

BAD POLITICIANS → BAD GOVERNMENT

Same thing when our job sucks. Blame the boss:

BAD BOSS → BAD JOB

We can explain almost anything this way. It's familiar and doesn't overtax our thinking. It's reassuring too. When

**L'Express*, "Les circuits effarants de l'argent en Corse" (The incredible money circuits in Corsica)," June 18, 1998, pp. 64–70.

things go wrong, it's not our fault. This kind of thinking works fairly well for many of life's everyday problems. Here's a simple example. Why, wonders a distraught mother, has an ugly gash suddenly appeared in the dining room table? "Tommy did it," says her daughter, smiling brightly. "He was working on his model plane."

TOMMY'S SCREW-UP → DAMAGED TABLE

The gash in the table aligns with a basic, everyday way of explaining things that go wrong. We'll call it "simple thinking," to distinguish it from systems thinking. It's built around four simple assumptions:

1. *When things go wrong, someone is at fault.* The culprit was too clumsy, short-sighted, stupid, or selfish to do things right. The gash wouldn't be there without Tommy's slip-up. We all learned as children the importance of assigning blame for every scarred table, stained carpet, or wounded sibling. Pinpointing who is at fault is comforting. In one stroke it resolves ambiguity, explains mystery, and makes clear the next step: Punish the guilty.

2. *The culprit isn't us.* Like most of us, Tommy's sister understood the importance of staying out of blame's way. She moved quickly to shift the spotlight somewhere else. Tommy knew this, too. He'd long since fled the scene.

3. *Cause and effect are near neighbors.* Knife slips. Gash appears instantly, right at the point of impact. Much of life seems to work this way. Suppose it's early morning and time to start another exciting workday. You hear the alarm, groan, and bat it. It falls silent. You fumble for the light switch. Visibility improves. You stumble down the stairs and hit the

button on the coffee maker. You soon have a cup of bracing brew. Your day is moving onto a higher plane. Action led to predictable reaction every step of the way.

4. *Causality travels on one-way streets.* Clearly, the knife caused the gash. It makes no sense to say "the gash caused the knife" or "the gash made the knife do it." The knife was cause. The gash was effect. That's all there is to it.

This kind of simple thinking works okay for life's easier hurdles and mishaps. It helps us avoid unpleasant surprises and embarrassing moments. But it leads us astray for many of the harder—and more important—problems. These require understanding complex relationships among multiple things—in other words, systems. It would be nice if systems weren't so complicated. But pretending they're easy doesn't make them so. It just gets us in trouble. Systems are complicated because they consist of multiple parts and because the parts influence one another in complex ways. Some systems are very large, like the global economy or the Earth's environment. Others, like the last virus that laid you up for a few days, are very small. In the social world, systems range from large societies, governments, and multinational corporations down to nuclear families and even dating couples. Since we've all had experience in families, we'll use a fairly simple example to illustrate basic ideas about how systems work. Join us for a small slice of everyday life in a midwestern family. The cast has four characters: Dad (Lee), Mom (Joan), older son (Chris), and younger son (Brad). Actually, five if you count the dog (a Dalmatian named Van Gogh). At first glance, you may only see a mundane story of four people stumbling through breakfast. Look deeper, and you'll begin to see system dynamics at work.

THE CASE OF THE SULLEN SON

The alarm rings at 7:30, and Lee reluctantly wakes up. Joan asks him to get the boys up so both can get to camp on time. She heads for the shower. Lee tries to wake Brad, who groans, "N-o-o! N-o-o!" Lee gets about the same response from Chris. Lee goes downstairs, walks and feeds the dog, and brings in the newspapers. Brad wanders into the kitchen and turns on the television to watch *Little Bear*, a favorite morning program. Lee asks Brad what he wants for breakfast. No answer. Lee repeats the question several times. He is finally rewarded with a loud, impatient reply of "Cereal!!"

Lee, fairly calmly, replies, "Try that again."

Brad responds, more softly, "Please."

"Which cereal?" No response. Lee persists. "What cereal do you want?"

"Rice Krispies!" comes the loud and irritated reply.

Older brother Chris, who has just entered the kitchen and started to get his own breakfast, says, "You're a little out of control, Brad."

Brad falls silent. Lee gets the cereal and squeezes orange juice. Joan comes into the kitchen and says hello to everyone. Lee and Joan discuss the day's schedule. Joan works on assembling lunches, water bottles, and assorted camp necessities. Lee starts his morning exercise on a stationary ski machine. After a few minutes he interrupts his regimen to put sunscreen on Brad. Brad shouts, "No-o-o! I don't want suntan lotion." After further negotiation, Lee eventually succeeds in applying the lotion. He then drives Brad to soccer camp. Soon after, Joan drives off in a different direction to deposit Chris at basketball camp, before going on to her office. Meanwhile, Lee returns home, finishes his exercise, and eats breakfast. He notes that it's 10:30 and wonders how he could have been up three hours while getting so little done.

Pretty ordinary stuff. It happens all the time. But there's a system at work here. Most often, whether we're at home or at work, we don't notice system dynamics. We just slide quickly into simple thinking. Usually with dismal results. Systems thinking can make a big difference by helping us see more deeply and identify better options. We'll see some of the possibilities as we entertain the question: Why was Brad so grumpy?

Simple thinking: *Look for someone to blame.*
Systems thinking: *The system did it.*

An easy response to any problem is to find a culprit to blame. If Brad's grumpy, let's pin the rap on him. Then we can start crabbing, criticizing, threatening, yelling. If things go downhill too far, we may even resort to force or violence. The result is degenerating tailspins. A better alternative is to ask what's happening in the family system that might account for Brad's grumpiness.

Simple thinking: *It's not my fault.*
Systems thinking: *We're all part of the system.*

Once the blame game takes off, the family turns into a posse of prosecutors in search of a perpetrator. Before long, everyone feels wounded by unfair criticism. The typical result is alternating warfare and stalemate, along with a lot of pain and distress. To break the pattern, individuals need to get beyond blaming and acknowledge, "We're all part of the system, so we all need to be part of the solution." In the case at hand, Brad's parents and brother have to ask themselves what they might have contributed to the family's dysfunction.

Simple thinking: *Cause and effect are near neighbors.*
Systems thinking: *Cause and effect may be separated in time and space.*

Simple thinking leads us to look for the cause close to the effect. If Brad is grumpy, it must be his fault. Maybe he's in a bad mood. Maybe he has a personality defect.

BRAD'S DEFECTS → GRUMPINESS

An easy explanation, but it doesn't help much.

Simple thinking: *Causality travels down one-way streets.*
Systems thinking: *Causality moves in spirals.*

We won't see the system's dynamics without looking for a spiral of causality. We can start by looking at the events leading up to this particular morning. We'd learn that Brad was normally a cheerful and self-sufficient early riser. But an unusually hectic and complicated summer schedule of camps and classes had left him chronically tired and uncharacteristically grumpy. Who put the schedule together? His parents. They hoped to keep him busy and entertained so they could get on with their respective jobs. They'd have preferred a simpler schedule, but couldn't work one out. So they developed a convoluted program. Maybe zoo camp in the morning, followed by a quick sandwich in the car while en route to a computer class. At first, it seemed to work. Brad liked most of the activities. But there was an unanticipated cost. He was exhausted. So were his harried parents and brother. System meltdown, not individual moodiness, was the story's real villain.

FRANK 'N' HOPE: *BLAMING*

Hope: How's it going at your house, Frank?

Frank: Don't ask.

Hope: Of course, you're always grumping about your wife's moods.

Frank: So? She's moody.

Hope: Maybe because she's surrounded by three kids and a grouchy husband?

Frank: You're blaming me?

Hope: No. But aren't you part of the family too?

Frank: So's the dog, but he gets better treatment than I do.

Brad's case is an everyday example of how easy it is to fall into systems traps—at home as well as at work. To avoid such traps, we need to understand the systems dynamics that create them. Simple thinking won't do it. To learn systems thinking, follow six basic guidelines:

1. *Map the system.* You can learn a lot about a system by drawing a diagram of how key factors influence one another. In the case of the sullen son, start with the idea that causality moves in spirals rather than straight lines. That's basic to sys-

tems thinking. Next, make a list of the most important elements in the situation. Prune the list to make it as simple as possible without cutting out anything important. After that, try to diagram the interplay among the parts. Be playful. Try different combinations until the picture makes sense. If we apply this procedure to Brad's case, we might produce something like the diagram in Figure 2-1.

To read the diagram, start at the top—"pressures on parents." A causal arrow runs from there to "Brad's hectic schedule." Summers can be tough for two-career families. The original pressures caused, or helped to cause, the hectic schedule. Two causal arrows lead from the hectic schedule. One leads to Brad's feeling exhausted. The second heads right back to pressures on parents. The schedule achieved its goal; it kept the kids occupied. But it also created some unintended consequences. Mom and Dad had to expend lots

Figure 2-1. Grumpiness diagram.

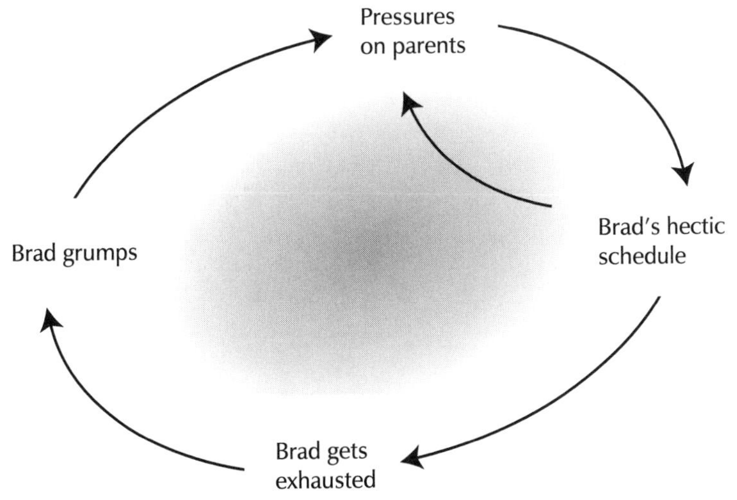

of time and energy coordinating the schedule and serving as chauffeurs. In addition, exhaustion made Brad grumpy, which put even more pressure on his parents.

This kind of mapping can make a big difference when you're dealing with a chronic problem that never seems to get any better regardless of what you do. Systems diagrams can help you pinpoint the real problem and identify options for improvement. Mapping also helps when you encounter puzzles or messes: You know something's wrong, but it's tough to figure out the underlying causes. Get a fresh pad of paper and start doodling—sketching alternative maps of the causal circles involved.

How do you know when you've got the right map? A good map suggests new possibilities for what's really going on and what to do next. A first indication is the "Aha!" test. If things seem clearer, and you're getting new insights, you're probably on the right track. The acid test is whether you're now able to solve the problem. If your diagram leads you to a new approach that works, it did its job.

2. *Look for high leverage.* In the pressures of the moment, it was tempting for Brad's semifrantic parents to punish him for his bad attitude and crummy behavior. We've seen it happen, and may remember falling into similar traps. But the systems diagram says there's little leverage in blaming. It only adds insult to injury. Brad's parents would be better off doing something about the hectic schedule or dealing differently with the pressures that caused it. When we misunderstand the system, we bog down in low-leverage strategies. We read diet books but never lose weight. We criticize kids for messy rooms, but the clutter persists. Low-leverage strategies are just as common at work. Some of the classics include:

- Constantly criticizing your staff and then wondering why performance never improves

- Hoping to boost sales of a flawed product by pumping more money into marketing
- Trying to jack up profits by cutting corners on quality

At home or work, when our current strategy is getting us nowhere, it's time to look for higher-leverage.

3. *Expect the unexpected.* Feedback loops are a basic feature of systems, but they're not always obvious. In Brad's case, no one anticipated that a schedule designed to make parents' life simpler would ultimately generate more overload. In a business example of the same phenomenon, a software firm's rush to ship a new product was delayed by a myriad of "bugs." To address the problem, management offered programmers cash incentives for every bug they identified. A classic example of simple thinking:

CASH REWARDS → PROGRAMMERS FIND MORE BUGS → FEWER BUGS

It worked great at first. The programmers tracked down bugs with a vengeance. Trouble was, they got hooked on the extra dough. When bugs began to dry up, the coders had to create new ones to keep the cash flowing. A barter system sprung up: "You create a bug for me, and I'll make one for you." If you try to diagram the system, you might get something like the diagram in Figure 2-2.

It's easy to blame management for being short-sighted or programmers for being greedy. But that's just more simple thinking. Both were part of the same system. The incentives worked: They motivated coders to find glitches. The problem was an unexpected feedback loop. Finding bugs got you more cash but it reduced the number of remaining bugs. So the coders had an incentive to generate new glitches to keep

Figure 2-2. Bug market.

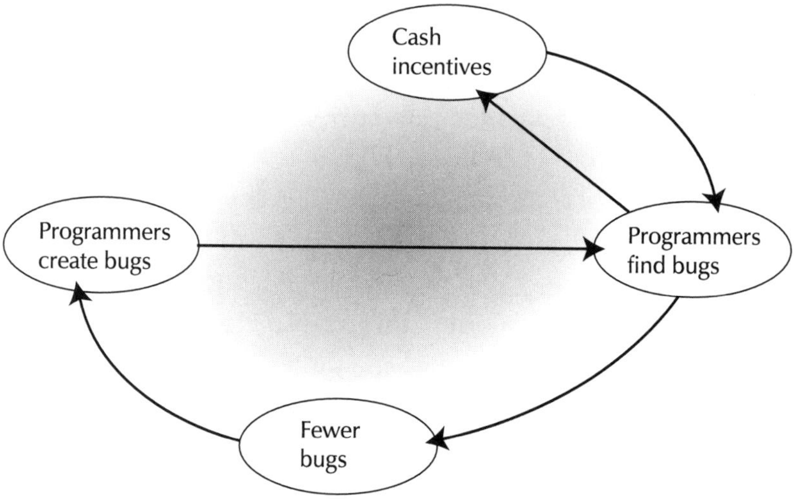

the dollars flowing. Had managers anticipated the extra loop, they'd have realized that the rewards would turn into an expensive distraction that focused workers on solving the wrong problem.

We fall into hidden loop traps when our actions trigger unanticipated feedback spirals that steer the system in the wrong direction. As another example, take the effort of a big U.S. city to increase the productivity of its garbage haulers with better performance measures. It seemed simple: Set tonnage standards and weigh trucks at the beginning and end of the workday. Once again, simple thinking led to undesirable results. Enterprising employees figured out that a hose hooked to a hydrant was a quick and easy way to get the tonnage up. Water's heavy, and you can pour it on a lot faster than you can pick up its weight in garbage. Trouble was, heavier, wetter trash didn't figure in the department's mission statement.

FRANK 'N' HOPE: *WATERING GARBAGE*

Frank: The key to success. Fudge the numbers.

Hope: What's it do for customers?

Frank: You take care of customers. I'll keep the boss happy. We'll see who gets ahead.

Hope: How's anyone gonna get ahead if we all go down the tubes?

Frank: Beats me. Not my job. But I've been here a long time. What about you?

4. *Allow for delays and "sleeper effects."* Things get even trickier in systems with delays and time lags. Let's revise Brad's grumpiness diagram by adding a couple of delays, as shown in Figure 2-3. The hectic schedule didn't affect Brad

Figure 2-3. Delayed grumpiness diagram.

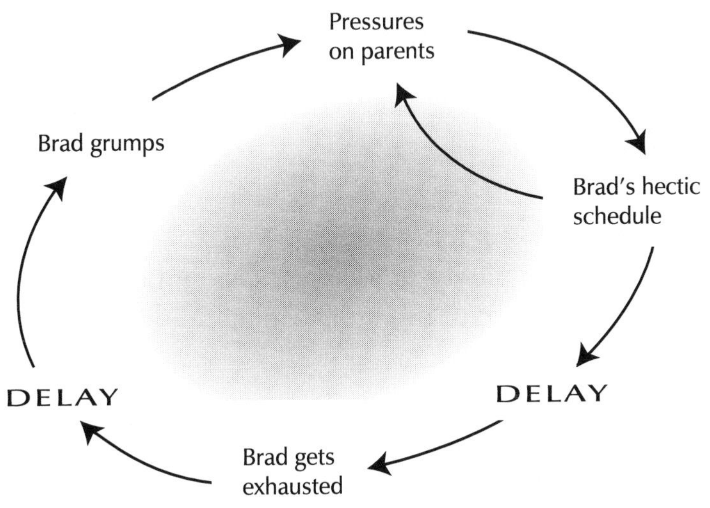

right away. At first it seemed to be a big success. Brad liked the variety and excitement. It took a few weeks before the grind wore him down, and even more time before grumpiness erupted full force. Delays between cause and effect make things hard because of a basic limitation in human learning. We're efficient at making connections when cause and effect are closely linked. When they're separated, it's much harder to figure out what caused what. Brad's grumpiness broke out long after the summer schedule went into effect, and a week or two after he started to show signs of exhaustion. This made it harder for his frazzled parents to see the scheduling-moodiness connection.

For a business example, take the notorious case of "Chainsaw Al" Dunlap.* For a while, at least, he was a hero of corporate downsizing. During his tenure as chief executive of Scott Paper, Dunlap more than doubled profits and market value. His strategy? Cut people—half the managers, half of research and development, and one-fifth of blue-collar workers. Short-term financial outcomes were impressive, but employee morale sank and Scott lost market share in every major product line. Dunlap didn't stick around long enough to find out if he'd sacrificed Scott's future for short-term gains. After less than two years on the job, he sold the company to its biggest competitor. Dunlap walked away with almost $100 million for his efforts. Then he wrote a best-selling book, *Mean Business*, to promote his gospel: Much of American business needed to be "Dunlapped."

There were plenty of believers, including the Sunbeam Corporation's board of directors. They hired Dunlap in mid-

*The story of Al Dunlap was compiled form J. A. Byrne, "How Al Dunlap Self-Destructed," *Business Week*, July 6, 1998, pp. 58–65 and Dana Canedy, "Sunbeam's Board, in Revolt, Ousts Job-Cutting Chairman," *The New York Times*, June 16, 1998, pp. A-1 and D-2.

1996 to work his managerial magic on their struggling appliance business. Initially, it looked like a brilliant move: The stock price jumped 50 percent the day Dunlap was hired. Dunlap promised 20 percent annual gains in revenues and profits. He started with a bang by laying off more than 18,000 workers. For more than a year, Dunlap's strategy seemed to work. In fact, it actually worked too well. Sunbeam's stock soared so high Dunlap couldn't follow his usual script: Sell the company at a high price and get out. No buyers were willing to pay what the market said Sunbeam was worth. So Dunlap had to stick around and manage the company. Things started to fall apart. To prop up the company's 1997 numbers, Dunlap's minions pushed off-season merchandise out the door. They offered discounted, buy-now-pay-later prices on electric blankets in the summer and barbecue grills in December. Mortgaging future sales only delayed the inevitable: a big splash of red ink. And a free fall in the stock price early in 1998. Dunlap, despite his self-description as "Rambo in pin stripes," tried to blame El Niño and assorted enemies. His board didn't buy it. They sacked him less than two years after he came aboard.

Al Dunlap was by no means the first—nor the last—manager to build a career by maximizing production of golden eggs while slowly suffocating the goose. In organizations, and in life, there are many examples of actions that look good short-term but turn sour in the long run. A systems model might look like the one in Figure 2-4.

The strategy might be slash and burn à la Dunlap, drinking martinis to relieve stress, offering big rebates to get customers to buy now, or borrowing from a loan shark to pay off your gambling debts. In each case, the strategy seems to work short-term. The long-term costs only become apparent

Figure 2-4. The time-lag trap.

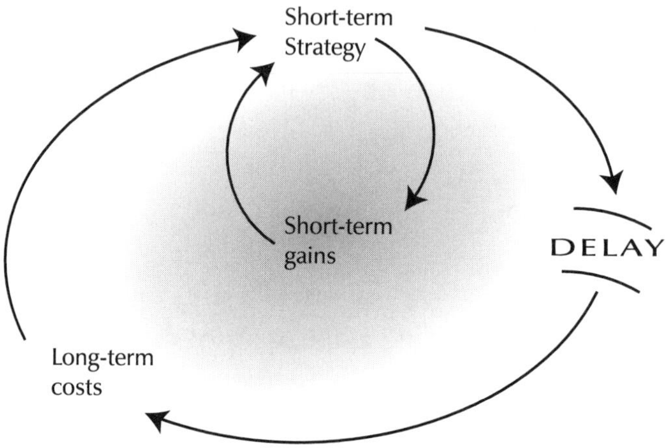

farther down the road: alcoholism, red ink, or threats of bodily harm.

5. *If you hit a tar baby, stop pounding.* In Joel Chandler Harris's famous fable, Brer Fox created a tar baby to trap his archenemy, Brer Rabbit. Hopping happily down the road, the amiable rabbit encountered the newcomer and greeted him politely. The tar baby's rude nonresponse came as a surprise. Brer Rabbit made repeated overtures, but the tar baby remained stubbornly unresponsive. Finally, he lost his cool. He started thumping the tar baby to teach him some manners. Bad idea. The harder Brer Rabbit hit, the more stuck he got. He kept pounding until he was buried in tar. In his book *The Fifth Discipline: The Art and Practice of the Learning Organization* (New York: Doubleday/Currency, 1990), Peter Senge captures the same phenomenon in his principle that "the harder you push, the harder the system pushes back."

Systems absorb energy like tar babies because they're filled with devices that work like thermostats. The devices are programmed to keep things at a preset level. They intervene tirelessly to eliminate deviations from the norm. The moral: Don't fight the thermostats. Instead, figure out where they are and look for ways to reset them. In Brad's case, it was tempting for the parents to view Brad as an uncongenial tar baby and start pounding on him (not physically—they're modern, middle-class parents) by blaming and shaming. Yet, if the parents' schedule created the problem, punishing Brad would have been a classic case of blaming the victim. A surefire way to make a bad situation worse.

6. *Don't be seduced by illusions.* It's easy to be deceived by subtle events that don't conform to commonsense thinking. When we're fooled, we often leap to illusions. Two old Sufi stories about the wise-fool, Mullah Nasrudin, illustrate the dangers. In the first, a neighbor encounters Nasrudin throwing bread crumbs around his house. The following dialogue ensues:

> NEIGHBOR: Feeding the birds?
> NASRUDIN: No. Keeping the lions away.
> NEIGHBOR: But there are no lions around here!
> NASRUDIN: Exactly. Effective, isn't it?

In the second, Nasrudin was wandering home on a moonlit night after an evening of revels. Chancing to look down a well, he saw the moon beaming back at him. "I've got to get the moon back where it belongs," he thought to himself. He dropped a rope into the well, hoping to snag the moon, and began to pull on it. At first the rope caught on a rock, and Nasrudin couldn't budge it. As he continued to tug, the rock suddenly released. Nasrudin found himself sprawled on his back, still holding the rope. Looking up, he saw the moon in its usual spot. "Good thing I came along, isn't it?" said he with a smile of triumph.

It's easy to spot the fallacies in repelling lions with bread crumbs or moving the moon with a rope. But similarly convoluted thinking misleads us all the time. Brad's parents, for example, could easily invent a variety of explanations for his grumpiness. "That TV show he watched last night upset him. Let's cut back on TV." "He been eating too much sugar. Let's cut back on desserts." If they cut back on TV or desserts, and Brad happened to be less grumpy the next morning, they could be tricked by an illusion as sensible as Nasrudin's notions about bread crumbs or the moon.

Similar things happen regularly at work. Suppose, for example, that your boss gets transferred, and you figure you should get her job. But the promotion goes to Pat instead. Since you're sure Pat doesn't merit the job nearly as much as you do, she must be kissing up. Could be, but more likely you just latched onto an illusion. It's comforting. It establishes that you were screwed out of a promotion you really deserved. A remarkable thing about this kind of thinking is that it works for all times and situations, no matter what the outcome is. Suppose you work hard on promoting a new product, and sales are even better than expected. Naturally, you figure you did great work. However, if sales disappoint, you can still figure that you did great work, but the engineers gave you a bad product. Or the timing was bad, or market conditions were worse than anyone could have predicted. Pick the most comforting illusion. It's always dangerous to grab the first plausible explanation, instead of reviewing our assumptions to make sure we're not kidding ourselves.

ESCAPING CLUELESSNESS II: MAPPING THE SYSTEM

COMMON SENSE OFTEN LEADS TO SIMPLE THINKING:

- LOOK FOR SOMEONE TO BLAME.
- EXPECT CAUSE CLOSE TO EFFECT.
- COUNT ON ONE-WAY, STRAIGHT-LINE CAUSALITY.

SYSTEMS THINKING TEACHES US TO:

- DEVELOP SYSTEMS DIAGRAMS.
- LOOK FOR HIGH LEVERAGE.
- EXPECT THE UNEXPECTED.
- ALLOW FOR SLEEPER EFFECTS.
- STOP POUNDING WHEN WE HIT A TAR BABY.
- AVOID LEAPING TO ILLUSIONS.

Looking Ahead

- If simplistic thinking gets us in trouble now, we ain't seen nothing yet.
- Change will come even faster in the future, and workplaces will keep getting more complicated.
- If we don't get smarter about systems:
  —We'll be even more confused.
  —Our effectiveness will go down, and stress will go up.

SUGGESTIONS FOR FURTHER READING

Chapters 1 to 5 in Peter Senge's *The Fifth Discipline* provide one of the best introductions to systems and systems thinking, and their importance to an organization's ability to learn. Some readers find that Senge's more recent book, *The Fifth Discipline Fieldbook: Tools for Building a Learning Organization*, is even more readable and practical. Barry Oshry's *Seeing Systems* provides a very different, but provocative perspective on understanding system dynamics. (We discuss some of Oshry's ideas in Chapter 7.)

See the Bibliography for publication details of these books.

PART II

ORGANIZATIONAL POLITICS EXPLAINED

3

PLAYING THE GAME WITHOUT GETTING EATEN

Politics at work are as certain as death and taxes. Things make better sense and we can accomplish more if we understand political games and learn to play with the pros. In the next two chapters we cover the basics of getting things done without getting done in. This chapter looks at the first step in political effectiveness: mapping the political terrain. In Chapter 4 we look at how to get and use power.

Around the world, people hate politics, particularly office politics. In television and films, books and comic strips, business executives are repeatedly portrayed as heartless, scheming predators who stop at nothing to amass greater wealth and power. On the list is the ruthless media baron in the classic *Citizen Kane*, routinely voted as the greatest movie ever made. The list also includes more forgettable films like *L.A. Confidential*, in which the genial chief of the Los Angeles police department turns out to be a murderous mobster, or the law office from hell in *The Firm* (based on John Grisham's novel of the same title).

FRANK 'N' HOPE: *OFFICE POLITICS*

Hope:	I don't want to be a politician. I just want to get some work done.
Frank:	You're a babe in the woods. You'll get eaten alive.
Hope:	That's the male model. Life is a football game. Winners and losers. Lots of casualties.
Frank:	You're living in a romance novel.
Hope:	Well, I'll never mistake you for Prince Charming.
Frank:	Good. There's no prince around here to save you. It's the real world. Play the game, or they'll carry you off the field.

Most organizations abound with tales of bosses' insensitivity, tirades, and humiliation of others. No matter what your job, it always seems as if someone else has more clout, and you're ten watts shy of enough power to light a small bulb. That wouldn't be so bad if you could count on the heavyweights to look out for your interests. But, surprisingly, they often seem to care more about their concerns than yours. Sometimes you feel surrounded by slugs and thugs, making it tough to stay above the slime. Here's an example:

Linda was a young fast-tracker in a big consumer products company. Only a few years out of business school, she'd already caught the eye of senior managers. Everyone predicted a stellar career. She was soon put in charge of a hot new product. To her delight, the initial rollout was a sensation. Her bubble burst when Linda got wind of a well-hidden report from company labs. Its data showed her product was going to make some users sick. Not a lot of them—only a small percentage, and only after they'd used the stuff for a while. Still, Linda was stunned. She'd read some magnificent phrases about integrity and safety in the company's ethics statement. So she figured her boss would want to do the right thing. She laid it on the line: They had to pull the product and fix the problem. To her surprise, the boss responded by reminding her of the millions they'd already plunked down. "But," said Linda, "what about the ethics statement? Nothing's more important than safety." Her boss took offense at the implication that he or anyone else would dream of doing anything unethical. After that, the conversation slid downhill fast.

In the following weeks, Linda continued to push for a recall. Her boss just became more defensive and annoyed. Finally, she got the bad news. "Sorry," he said. "But we've had to make a difficult decision. We feel you're letting personal feelings cloud your judgment. You're not providing the vision and leadership that this product needs. But we're offering you a very generous severance package."

Linda stared in disbelief at her boss. She'd thought things like this only happened in the movies. It took her months to get over the shock. She finally took off in search of a new career, but still carried the scars.

How do we make sense of Linda's misadventure? It's tempting, but too easy, to conclude that her bosses were thugs—unethical hypocrites who used their power to suppress the truth and kick her out. It's a convenient explanation whenever we run into arrogance and selfishness. Not all wrong, but not the whole story. It's another example of simplistic thinking—blaming individuals instead of understanding what's really going on. Even worse, it leaves us clueless about next steps. We may think we've explained things even though we have no inkling of what to do next.

Even if Linda's boss was a moral midget, there was still a bigger issue. He and Linda were both mired in a political mess. Neither knew a way out. Linda had stumbled onto a big problem. If she were politically alert, she wouldn't have needed a large neon sign flashing, "Danger! Political minefield ahead!" She'd have guessed that the report was hidden for a reason. Someone high up, maybe a top executive group, had decided to plunge forward despite the risks. Maybe her boss was in on the decision. Maybe he was just following orders. Whatever. It's always hazardous to plunge into a political minefield if you don't know where the explosives are buried. Linda needed better intelligence, and her boss was potentially a key source of information. But, as many subordinates would do in such a situation, she dumped everything in her boss's lap—"Here's the problem, big guy. You fix it." Not surprisingly, her boss panicked. Not because he was a psychopath. Deep down, he didn't really want to sell a dangerous product. But he felt trapped. He flailed around to find a way out—anything that wouldn't make him look bad or derail his promising career.

Linda didn't get it. She figured the boss didn't understand the situation's seriousness. So she pushed harder. She didn't see the obvious: The more she pushed, the more he dug in. Put yourself in the boss's shoes. How easy would it be for you to say something like, "What a mess! I don't want to peddle something that'll make people sick. But this product could make a lot of money, and my boss doesn't want to hear about health risks. If we pull the sucker, I'll lose my bonus, look like a dork, and get blown off the fast track. I don't have the foggiest idea what to do." So he tried to bury the mess and cover his tail by throwing Linda overboard. He hoped the problem would go away. Too late, he relearned the moral of the 1970s' Watergate scandal: It ain't the mistake, it's the cover-up that kills you. It's a tough lesson to learn. In 1998, "Monicagate" made it clear that even the White House hadn't fully absorbed it. The litany of catastrophe for Linda's company included sick customers, bad press, lawsuits, and a bunch of careers down the tubes. One of the major casualties was Linda's old boss.

Another depressing glimpse of corporate warfare. Linda's story isn't unique. We've seen worse. Whistle-blowers are regularly thrown to the sharks. Employees who complain about discrimination or sexual harassment typically encounter deafness and blindness. Organizations are inevitably jungles—alive with different species each competing for its share of scarce resources. As Woody Allen once observed, the lion may lie down with the lamb, but the lamb probably won't get much sleep. This stark reality makes it easy to become jaded and cynical. But that's just as short-sighted as being naive and gullible. Folks at work aren't always as evil as they seem. Nor as powerful. They're a lot like the rest of us: trying to pick their way through the minefields without getting blown up. Survival requires a good mine detector or a reliable map. As you get smarter about workplace politics, you start to see a lot more possibilities.

FRANK 'N' HOPE: *A PONY IN THE MANURE?*

Frank: You're a lot like Linda.

Hope: We're both female?

Frank: Yeah. And you both expect a pony in every manure pile.

Hope: Not always. But if there's one there, I'll find it!

Frank: Naah! You'll just spend your life covered in dung. Like Linda.

Hope: You missed the point, Frank. Linda was long gone when the outhouse blew. It was her bosses who wound up buried in doodoo.

We're all political animals. Little kids learn how to build coalitions and use power to get their way. They learn that sweet-talking grandpa or throwing a tantrum in a toy store often gets them what they want. Politics are a daily reality in every human group. Not just because people are naturally selfish or looking out only for themselves. They often are, but even when they're not, they're still political for two basic reasons: (1) Individuals want different things and (2) a world of scarce resources makes it impossible for everyone to get everything they want. As a result, conflict reigns in every organization from families to the United Nations.

Conflict arises from three ways that people are different: personality (who they are), position (where they are), and group memberships (who their friends are). We're all familiar with personality quirks. They play a big role in disputes with relatives, friends, or coworkers. But position often looms larger than personality. Conflicts are built into relationships between parents and children, bosses and subordinates, vendors and customers, meter maids and motorists. Group memberships are a third powerful source of differences. White-collar or blue, lawyers or engineers, Republicans or Democrats, Hindus or Moslems, white or black, straight or gay, pro-life or pro-choice, and on it goes. Different groups have distinctive values, goals, interests, and ways. These differences continually collide in contests about whose interests and values will prevail.

Differences don't always lead to conflict. If you like to lead and your partner prefers to follow, you can dance beautifully together. The other fundamental source of conflict is scarce resources. Whenever you and someone else both want to eat from the same rice bowl, things heat up. If you're separated by a chasm of differences in interests and world-view, common ground can be almost impossible to find. Disputes take on theological overtones. It's like asking Baptists and Catholics to agree about papal authority. Logic and data fly out the window, and power becomes the dominant coin of the realm.

Power? Isn't that what grasping, selfish louts amass in order to enrich themselves and humiliate everyone else? It often is. History is filled with folks who used power in malicious, stupid, destructive ways—Hitler, Stalin, and Pol Pot, not to mention the boss who fired Linda. But power is vital for saints as well as sinners, to do good or to do evil. Gandhi, FDR, and Mother Teresa worked their miracles through power. Power is simply the ability to make things happen. Whatever you want, you'll need power to get it. Otherwise, you're counting on luck or prayer.

The problem is: Most of us hate politics. Or at least we claim to. We see politics as a dirty, underhanded business, reserved for scoundrels who cut shady deals in smoke-filled rooms. That's where a lot of us need an attitude adjustment. There's a middle road between muggers' alley and the yellow-brick road of gullibility. A workplace is not Mr. Rogers's neighborhood. We'd like to think that our readers are caring, sensitive, and ethical. Otherwise you'd all be reading books about eating with the sharks or climbing to the top over co-workers' battered bodies. But if good people avoid politics, thieves and con artists have an open field. Every day in any workplace, political games are in full swing. As soon as you arrive at work, you're in the game, whether you choose to suit up or sit out. If you're on the playing field with few skills and little clue about how the game works, your losses will make someone else's day. After a major initiative went awry, one executive ruefully told us, "I thought I'd covered all the bases. Then I realized everyone else was playing football." You have two choices. You can be the ball that everyone else kicks around. Or you can learn how to play with the pros. To do that you need to learn some basic rules for playing the political game:

1. *Map the minefield.* Political land mines are strewn here and there in most workplaces. A map of where they're buried can save you from painful surprises. A good political map answers three key questions: (1) Who are the players? (2) What does each one want? (3) Who's got clout? Start with a blank sheet of paper. Draw a line down the left side. Label it "high power" at the top, and "low power" at the bottom. Across the bottom draw another line. Put the label "allies" at the left, "fence-sitters" in the middle, and "opponents" at the right. Then identify the players (individuals or groups) and their positions on the field. We'll revisit Linda's case as an example. Figure 3-1 shows what Linda might have imagined when she first approached her boss. On this chart, the boss has no strong feelings about the decision to pull the product,

Figure 3-1. Linda's initial map.

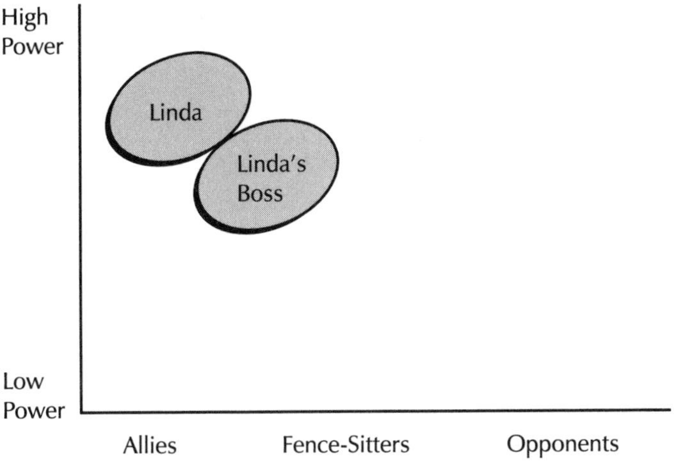

and the justice of her cause gives Linda enough power to convince him she's right.

Figure 3-2 shows a more realistic picture. Here, it's clear that the more Linda pushes her boss, the more he'll feel like an apple in a cider press. It's easy to see why the boss is tempted to deep-six Linda rather than confront the big guns pushing him from another direction.

If Linda had taken pencil to paper, would she have seen the second map? Maybe not. But the effort might have got her thinking: How much do I really know about the game? Do I have the power I need? If not, how could I get it? Have I identified all the key players? What are their motives and muscle? Good questions to ask whenever you try to chart situational politics. If you don't know the answers, it's time for some more spade work.

2. *Know when to hold and when to fold.* Would it have done any good if Linda had recognized the second map? Was she doomed to fail anyway? Maybe so. But at least she might

Figure 3-2. A more likely map.

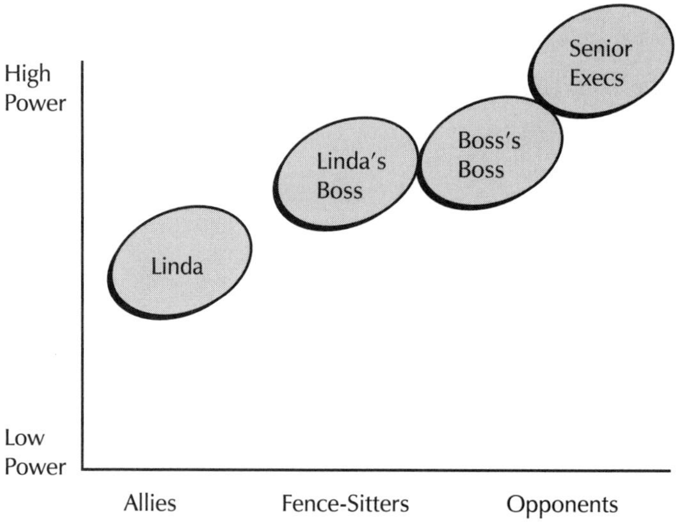

have made a more informed decision: "Do I really want my fragile career splattered over a no-win issue?" Laying down your life for your company is rarely a solid career move. You can do better. Cut your losses. Live to fight another day. Good poker players don't bet the farm on a losing hand. They wait for better cards.

Does that mean Linda should have chucked her ethics out the window, and colluded with a bad decision? No. Her bosses were headed for a wreck. Linda was smart not to hop on the train. The more important your cause, the more you need to find a viable strategy *before* you charge the hill. In both poker and business, hands that start weak don't always stay that way. Sometimes you can outdraw the opposition. Political dynamics are fluid. The terrain changes all the time. Linda was outgunned at the outset. But what if she could find some allies among the fence-sitters? Or defuse some of the opposition? Were there other players she could have drawn into the fray? Were there ways to induce her boss, or boss's boss, to rethink their strategic interests? Could she have helped the bosses see the impending train wreck? Linda's situation was tough, but not hopeless. To succeed, she needed political smarts and a better strategy. Above all, she needed to understand how to get and use power. So does everyone. We talk about how in Chapter 4.

ESCAPING CLUELESSNESS III: MAPPING THE POLITICAL TERRAIN

- ACCEPT POLITICAL REALITY.
- ASSESS THE INTERESTS AND CLOUT OF KEY PLAYERS.
- SEEK WAYS TO RALLY ALLIES, LURE FENCE-SITTERS, AND NEUTRALIZE OPPONENTS.
- PLAY STRONG HANDS; CUT YOUR LOSSES WITH WEAK ONES.

4

Power: Who You Are, Where You Are, and What You've Got

You've heard the cynical update of the golden rule many times: Those with the gold make the rules. Jaundiced, yes, but with a familiar grain of truth. Those with power tend to get what they want. Those without end up with leftovers. If you've been spending too much time at the back of the line, this chapter provides guidance on improving your odds.

Why do others always seem to have more clout? Partly, it's a mirage that comes from feeling one-down. We learn our first lessons about being a subordinate at our parents' knees. Early memories of dependence and helplessness linger for a long time. They lead us to overestimate our clout when we're top dog, and underestimate it when we're subordinates. Bosses often think they have more power than they do. After all, they can give orders, reward and punish, hire and fire. But employees have minds of their own. They don't always follow orders or kowtow to management's carrots and sticks. Power generates friction as soon as you try to use it. Firing people costs time, energy, and money. No matter how lofty your title, you're almost always hedged in by conflicting expectations. We sometimes imagine that CEOs are all-powerful. But they have to worry about board members, stock analysts, the media, shareholders, takeover specialists, politicians, regulators, customers, vendors, competitors, and employees. As subordinates we often feel we're at the bottom of a long food chain, with less power than a dead battery. But that's another illusion. Power takes many forms. There's almost always more available—if you know where to look.

Most kinds of power cluster around three things: who you are, where you are, and what you've got (summarized in Table 4-1). "Who you are" clout comes from your history and personal qualities. These include verbal skills, social graces, or compulsion to succeed—often acquired from family and friends. Equally important are information and know-how picked up at school or elsewhere, as well as career-building experiences in a variety of jobs. All these yield knowledge and skill—prime sources of power. In a knowledge society, a big chunk of social power is positioned right between people's ears. If you use your personal resources

Table 4-1. Sources of power.

Basic Sources of Power	*Examples*
Who you are (personal power)	Personal characteristics (charm, energy, etc.) Knowledge and skill Credibility (track record, reputation)
Where you are (position power)	Job or position Department or organization
What you've got (resource power)	Resources (money, information, favors, etc.) Friends and allies Coercive force

well over time, you build a track record that provides another key source of power—credibility. Think about actor Will Smith. At last notice he was pulling down upwards of $20 million a picture. Why? Because of his track record. His movies sell tickets. He's a magnet because moviegoers love him. He's the charming, funny, vulnerable, sexy, gutsy, rebellious, unsinkable male we'd like to be or be with.

Think about your own history. Do you consistently step up to challenges and deliver what you promise? Are people convinced they can trust what you say? A favorable history confers clout. It convinces people that you can shape a situation and deliver the goods. Think too about your personal qualities. What knowledge and skills have you mastered? We trust lawyers when we're sued and doctors when we're ill. We believe they know things we don't. Expertise is a wonderful source of power, and it's portable—you can take it anywhere. Think about people you admire, or people you'd go to for help. Do you have the qualities that you prize in them? If your family was debilitating, your school experience rocky, and your job history spotty, you've got a credibility deficit to overcome. Knowledge, skills, and track record take time to build. If you're holding a weak hand, it's time to get started on a more productive path.

Even if you've got the personal power of a beached tadpole, all is not lost. Another source of clout is being in the right place—the right job, a key department, or a rising enterprise. In every organization, some jobs or ranks carry more influence and control than others. Colonels outrank captains, and generals outrank colonels. But being in an elite unit can be as important as having a fancy title. For a time in the Reagan administration, Colonel Oliver North was more powerful than most generals because of his strategic White House location. If you found two messages in your voice mail, one from the White House and the other from the Bureau of Mines, which call would you return first? In every organization, some departments or units are more visible and powerful than others. Part of political savvy is recognizing and going where the leverage is better.

But what if you've got a lightweight job in a backwater unit? You're not out of the game yet. You can still capitalize on things you control—resources like money, information, and allies. Information is power everywhere. If you're good at keeping your ear to the ground and assembling stray bits of crucial data, people will seek you out. Friends, allies, and networks also yield enormous leverage. Nothing very big ever happens in organizations unless enough people from various roles and units join together to support it. Smart politicians systematically build relationships with key players; getting to know them, learning how they think and what they care about. As a young member of Congress, Lyndon Johnson began to assemble his power base by running errands for his senior colleagues. He developed a long list of grateful friends who owed him something. Many modern power brokers would experience a real dilemma if they had to choose between their first-born and their Rolodexes.

Subordinates can often exercise power through resources they control, particularly when they band together in groups. Slowdowns, sickouts, subtle sabotage, work-to-rule, and strikes all make the point that workers have muscle. One reason airline pilots are so well paid is that they can cripple a multibillion-dollar company just by staying home. Every few years, pilots at one carrier or another generate chaos and headlines with a strike or a sickout.

As you can see, power has many forms. You need to know how to get your share. Like most things in life, gaining power is a matter of discipline and focus. Hard work, persistence, and an agenda—a clear sense of what you want—will take you a long way. In building your agenda, you need to make some key choices. One is whether to look out only for your own interests or try to contribute to the collective good as well. This choice is not always easy, particularly if your workplace has the egalitarian charm and limited prospects of a leaky slave galley. If the boat is sinking, saving yourself may be a sensible choice. If your company treats you like dirt, or puts out goods and services that mostly make the world more miserable, job disgust is a sane and constructive sentiment. But ask if you really want to work for a place that delivers shoddy products or destructive services. If not, help your organization do better. Or go somewhere else.

Wherever you work, you can opt for one of four basic approaches to workplace politics, outlined in Table 4-2. You can be a victim (a bad choice, but victims are abundant), a good soldier (you'll be loyal and hardworking, but you may wind up giving a lot more than you get back), a pol (you might get rich and make it to the top, if your enemies don't torpedo you first), or a pro (a rare being who combines commitment with political savvy).

We all become victims from time to time, but it's pointless to spend your life as a self-centered doormat. The victim role is tragic and self-destructive. You're looking out mostly for yourself, but doing a poor job of it. You contribute little

Table 4-2. Political orientations.

Organizational Commitment	*Political Savvy*	
	Low (politically clueless)	*High (politically astute)*
High	Good Soldier	Pro
Low	Victim	Pol

to the organization but lack the punch to convince people otherwise. So you're written off as a shirker, a manipulator, or an egotist. Sooner or later you lose out to folks with more political savvy. You probably know some long-term victims. They're often bitter, disappointed people who feel the world's been terribly unfair to them. The boss in Linda's case wound up being a victim, even though Linda saw him as more like Darth Vader. The boss's response to Linda was heavy-handed and clumsy, a reliable sign of a political amateur. Linda offers one example of a classic good soldier: loyally trying to do what's best for the organization, but crippled by political naiveté. There were likely some smart pols lurking in the background, maneuvering her boss into the villain's role without leaving their fingerprints. Every organization has at least a few skillful pols. Some are infested with them. If you get in their way, pols can be dangerous and destructive. But if you can figure a way to align their interests with yours, you may leverage their skills and turn them into great allies. Dancing with wolves is risky business, but if you can get the pack on your side, they can be a lot of help.

FRANK 'N' HOPE: *VICTIM OR POL?*

Hope:	Why the smirk?
Frank:	I'm a pol on my way up. Forget this commitment B.S. Good soldiers get shot. But, when it's your turn, I'll send flowers.
Hope:	You're too kind. But if you're that smart, how come you're so far down the food chain?
Frank:	Bad luck. I''ve been screwed a few times.
Hope:	Isn't what what victims say?

In Linda's world, as in Dilbert's, the species that's hardest to spot is the pro: the rare individual who wants to make a real contribution and has enough political smarts to do it. Learn to be a pro. You'll likely add value to your organization and be amply rewarded in return. There's no danger that your workplace has an oversupply, so there won't be much competition. Not a bad deal. Win-win deals are a pro's specialty.

A BRIEF QUIZ ON POWER

Study the cartoon in Figure 4-1. Try to analyze both power and political stances for the three characters in the strip: Dilbert, Dogbert, and the "pointy-haired boss." Then answer the following two questions (preferably without peeking at the answers that follow):

1. Who's demonstrating, or not demonstrating, what kinds of power?
2. Which political stance does each character represent?

Figure 4-1. Dogbert offers a lesson on power.

In terms of power, you should have noted that Dogbert covers most of the bases. He claims power based on where he is in terms of both department (network services) and position ("emperor for life" is a gorgeous title). He's got the key resource of information and claims a very powerful ally in the board of directors. Personal power? Dogbert may not be the world's most lovable canine, but his admirably clear agenda and guilt-free ruthlessness could put him on a political fast track. The pointy-haired boss, on the other hand, illustrates that who you are can be a liability as well as an asset. A boss who hopes the escape key will produce a quick getaway is clearly not playing with a full deck. Dilbert, as usual, doesn't show much backbone. He may not be powerless, but there's no sign that he'll take advantage of whatever opportunities are at hand.

In terms of political acumen, Dogbert's awareness of multiple sources of power and ability to accumulate clout are classic indicators of a pol in action. There is one dissonant note. Outside a cartoon strip, smart pols would generally dispense with public arrogance. Once you're on top, why rile the locals unnecessarily? Meanwhile, Dilbert is glued to his desk, attending to this message from the top in classic good soldier fashion. The pointy-haired boss finds himself a victim: He's trying to look out for himself, but his strategy isn't equal to the task.

FRANK 'N' HOPE: *POWER FOR POWER'S SAKE*

Frank:	Love that Dogbert! My main man!
Hope:	You? More like Dilbert.
Frank:	You're just jealous. Dogbert's got the clout.
Hope:	Dogbert, maybe. But you?
Frank:	I'm working on it. One of these days I'll hit the big one.
Hope:	Not if it hits you first.

So how do you become a pro? There are five rules, including two you already know from the previous chapter: (1) Map the playing field, and (2) know when to hold and when to fold. Three more and you're ready to be a serious player.

3. *Know what you want and what you can get.* Reflecting on his experience as a college president, Warren Bennis in his book *Why Leaders Can't Lead: The Unconscious Conspiracy Continues* (San Francisco: Jossey-Bass, 1989), made a deceptively simple observation, "It struck me that I was most effective when I knew what I wanted." Sounds obvious, but it's harder than we'd like to think. A lot of times we're fuzzy or confused about what we really want. Maybe we don't like things as they are, and we'd like them to be better. But better how? One thing that separates pros from the rest of the pack is that they're clear and realistic about what they want. Clarity rarely comes in a sudden, blinding flash of insight. It's earned and learned. Pros use their knowledge of the playing field to identify players who can help them get clearer about

possibilities. They talk to people. They ask questions and test options. This is particularly important anytime you suspect your opponents might be stronger than you are. That means you need to do something to improve the odds before launching a full-scale assault. Talking to potential opponents—finding out what they want and how they think—may lead to new avenues and prospects. At best, it helps you develop a clear agenda and a strategy to achieve it. At worst, you might save yourself from wasting time, energy, and reputation on a fool's errand.

4. *Embrace your friends and befriend your enemies.* Pros understand that good ideas rarely win on their merits alone. You need allies and supporters to do or change much of anything in a workplace. Our friend Natasha, for example, couldn't understand why her company had no recycling program. Day after day, she fretted about the reams and reams of paper landing in dumpsters en route to landfills. Natasha's clerical job gave her about as much authority as a slice of stale bread. But she started using her break times to go around and talk to people. Her basic approach was always the same: "This bothers me. Does it bother you? What could we do about it?" People kept saying that recycling was a good idea, but "Bill will never buy it." Natasha realized that Bill could make or break her project. The word in the hallways was that Bill always said no to anything he hadn't thought of himself. After hesitating for a while, Natasha managed to get a small opening on Bill's crowded calendar. She didn't argue with Bill or try to sell him on the virtues of recycling. Instead, she focused on getting to know him and understanding his thinking. In a short-but-sweet meeting, Natasha learned that Bill might go along with recycling—*if* it didn't cost too much money or too much of his time. That was all Natasha needed. She and a couple of allies she'd cultivated contacted recycling companies. They developed a one-page proposal

showing that recycling was feasible and would pay for itself. Bill hemmed and hawed for a while, but finally bought it. Natasha was ecstatic. All that paper no longer wound up in landfills. The key for Natasha was befriending Bill, her most important potential enemy.

5. *Make win-win deals.* Political pros see no sense in generating unnecessary pain, anger, and enemies. Instead, they're always on the lookout for win-win scenarios. In their classic primer on negotiation, *Getting to Yes* (Boston: Houghton Mifflin, 1981), Roger Fisher and William Ury developed four rules of thumb for finding common ground. The first is to *separate the people from the problem.* Blaming, criticizing, and attacking other people wastes time and motivates them to thwart you instead of helping. Better to focus on solving problems and enlisting others' help where possible. The second rule is to *focus on interests, not positions.* For example, when Natasha first met with Bill, their positions were incompatible: She was a recycling zealot, and he was a skeptic. The meeting could easily have turned into a stalemate with both parties defending the correctness of their positions. But Natasha probed to get at Bill's underlying interests. She learned that Bill mostly cared about cost and effort. Armed with that knowledge, Natasha developed a proposal that Bill could buy.

The third rule of thumb is to *invent options for mutual gain.* Finding an option that was good for both her and Bill was critical to Natasha's success. When two parties have conflicting preferences, there's a problem unless they can be a little creative. Things generally go a lot better if they spend time finding better alternatives instead of arguing about who's right or wrong.

The fourth rule of thumb for getting to yes is to *insist on objective criteria.* This rule is particularly useful whenever you and someone else are trying to decide what's fair. How do you judge a fair price for a house, or a fair wage in a labor-management negotiation? In real estate transactions, for example, both parties typically look at the sales price for recent "comparables." In labor negotiations, both sides look at recent settlements in similar situations.

All four rules of thumb are guidelines for productive negotiation, pathways to win-win outcomes. They're not magical. They're often hard to apply and won't make every conflict disappear. Even highly skilled pros sometimes lose, or find themselves in long, tough negotiations. But they generally make more friends than enemies, and they get a reputation for being reasonable and credible. It pays off over the long haul.

Escaping Cluelessness IV: Getting a Bigger Slice of the Pie

- Understand three forms of power and get the ones you need:
  - Who you are
  - Where you are
  - What you've got
- Choose a stance:
  - Victim (an option for losers)
  - Good soldier (good for the company, bad for you)
  - Pol (you could hit it big, or take a big hit)
  - Pro (best long-term bet)
- Set your agenda and move ahead.
- Embrace allies and soothe enemies.

Looking Ahead

- We'll see more, not less, workplace politics in the future:
  - —Globalization will continue to increase competition.
  - —Flatter, more flexible organizations will put more players with more interests on the playing field.
- You'll be more successful and get more done if you find the fertile ground between political naiveté and mugger's alley.

SUGGESTIONS FOR FURTHER READING

If you're buried somewhere near the bottom of the management ladder, a pair of excellent and practical guides to power in the workplace are John Kotter's *Power and Influence: Beyond Formal Authority* and Jeff Pfeffer's *Managing with Power: Politics and Influence in Organizations.* If you're seriously disenfranchised, try Saul Alinsky's classic *Rules for Radicals.* Alinsky provides a provocative array of tools and techniques for cutting the powers-that-be down to size. You can't go wrong with Machiavelli's classic, *The Prince*—still famous after 500 years because it has a lot to say to anyone trying to understand power and politics. Even older, and some readers would say even better, is Sun Tzu's *The Art of War.* Many see it as the greatest book ever written on strategy and conflict.

See the Bibliography for publication details of these books.

PART III
PEOPLE AT WORK

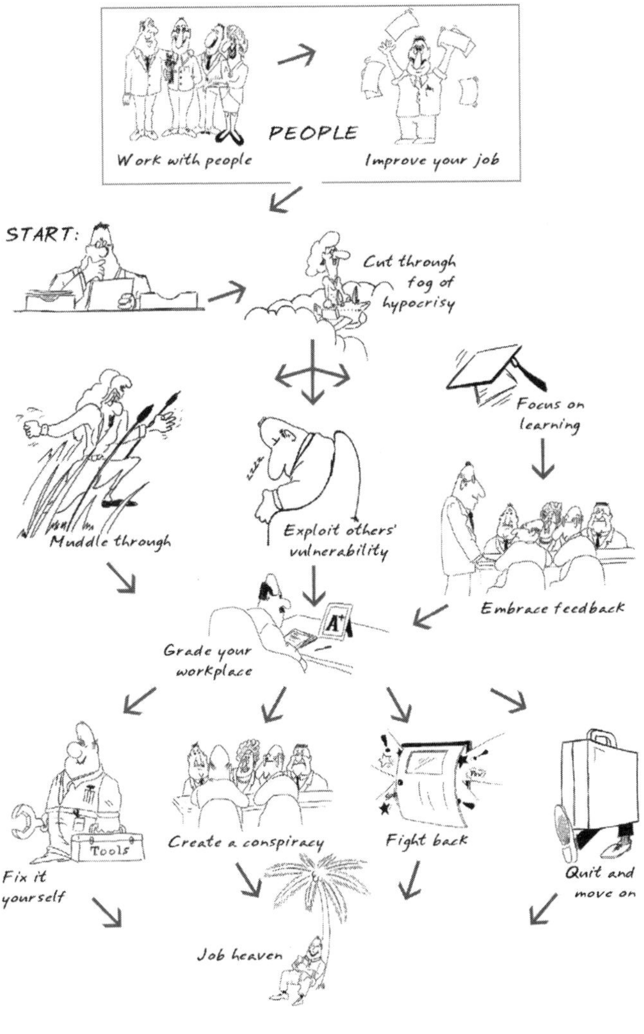

5

Improving Relationships at Work: Overcoming Blindness and Hypocrisy

We can't check our humanity at the door when we come to work. Needs and feelings, strengths and weaknesses, quirks and idiosyncrasies are always with us. That can work to your advantage if you understand yourselves and the people around you. It can be a disaster if you don't.

People often do strange and puzzling things at work. They hold grudges for years. They snipe at others behind their backs. They chronically say one thing and do another, oblivious to the hypocrisy of their ways. They screw up daily, but feel insulted by feedback and reject all offers of help or instruction. They keep rehashing the same tired clichés ("People are our most important asset," "Work smarter, not harder"), yet can't understand why everyone ignores them.

In this chapter we look more deeply into personal cluelessness—how being human often gets us in trouble at work. This has perplexed people since ancient times. Some 2,500 years ago, Lao-Tzu, a very wise Chinese philosopher, got to the heart of the issue: "Those who know others are wise. Those who know themselves are enlightened."* A similar point is made in the Christian Gospels, when Jesus says, "Why do you see the speck in your neighbor's eye, but not notice the log in your own? . . . You hypocrite, first take the log out of your own eye, and then you will see clearly to take the speck out of your neighbor's eye."† In the old days, the enlightened were scarce, and hypocrites were abundant. Look around your office. You may conclude that not much has changed.

Just to get by day to day, we all rely on a couple of dubious assumptions. The first is that we know what we're doing. The second is that we know what happens when we do it. These two assumptions fail a lot more than we realize. Too often, what we're really doing and what we think we're doing are as closely related as pigs and twigs. Freud confirmed it a century ago: People don't know their own minds. An ocean of research since has documented how much we're out of touch with our behavior and its impact.

If you accept that people are flying in the dark much of the time, the strange things they do make more sense. We've all been trained to say one thing and do another. We reach adulthood clinging to self-images poorly aligned to our actions. Education often magnifies the gaps. Business schools and management seminars, for example, try to teach otherwise sensible people to see themselves as skilled modern managers (SKIMMs). Even without such training, you can probably pass the brief SKIMM on the following pages. For each question, there are two possible replies. Only one represents the correct SKIMM self-image. Which is it?

*Quoted in T. Cleary, *The Essential Tao* (San Francisco: Harper, 1992), p. 29.
†Matthew 7:3–5.

1. As a SKIMM, do you:

   A. Encourage your staff to do whatever it takes to achieve outstanding business results by surprising and delighting the customer?

   B. Hover over your employees like a starving seagull to ensure that rules, policies, and procedures are scrupulously followed?

Easy, yes? Obviously, the correct image is A. All SKIMMs know they are supposed to be results-oriented, not petty bureaucrats. But try this one:

1a. As a SKIMM, what do you do when one of your subordinates bends a rule or diverges from company policy?

   A. Warmly congratulate the offender for focusing on results, not petty bureaucratic restrictions.

   B. Call the miscreant into your office, express your deep disappointment, and extract a promise that it will never happen again.

As you probably recognized, even dedicated pursuers of excellence have difficulty living up to the SKIMM creed when others stray from the straight and narrow. B is the more likely response, even if it violates tenets of modern management.

Let's try another one.

2. As a SKIMM, do you:

   A. Treasure subordinates, welcome their input, and try to empower them as much as possible?

   B. Pretend to listen while making all decisions yourself?

Once again, almost too easy. The correct image for SKIMMs is definitely A. BUT . . .

2a. As a SKIMM, what do you do when newly empowered subordinates start down a path that might not produce the results you want?

A. Step up your efforts at listening and empowerment?
B. Intervene at the speed of light to get folks back on the right track?

Here, too, the SKIMM credo is easier to preach than to practice. Under the pressures of managerial life, B is a more likely response. Notice the pattern here: SKIMMs have learned to hold an attractive image of themselves. Then they ignore their self-image when it's convenient to behave otherwise. But it's not just them. It's all of us. A family example lets us take a similar look at SKIMPS (skilled modern parents).

3. As a SKIMP, do you teach your children that:

A. They should be honest and truthful, maintaining their integrity even when the going gets tough.
B. They should lie strategically whenever it's more convenient.

Another easy one: the answer, of course, is A. Only deviants and psychopaths would train their children to be strategic liars. BUT . . .

2a. As a SKIMP, what do you do when your child accurately reports to your dinner guests, "Daddy says when you come over you drink too much and act weird."

A. Say, "We're so proud of you for telling the truth."
B. Silence the child with a cold stare, assure the guests that your child is delusional, change the subject as fast as possible, and (optional) pour everyone a really big drink.

FRANK 'N' HOPE: *BLIND HYPOCRISY*

Frank:	You want a hypocrite, look at my boss.
Hope:	How's he different from you?
Frank:	I practice what I preach.
Hope:	How come people say that you suck up and pound down?
Frank:	Who said that?
Hope:	I have to protect my sources. But try talking to some of your people once in a while.

The key point is that we're all trained to build a self-image grounded in fashionable virtues. We cling to these saintly self-images because they're our ticket to getting others' respect and to maintaining our own self-respect. But daily life presents situations where acting on virtue is challenging, or at least inconvenient. If we held to our espoused values, we might not get what we want. Worse, we'd feel vulnerable and threatened. So we often let virtue take a backseat to self-interest. It works. It gets us through most of life's routine challenges without too much pain and suffering. To *notice* that we are regularly inconsistent would be awkward. We'd feel dishonest or devious. So we gloss over inconsistencies and pat ourselves on the back for being realistic and practical.

At first glance, it might seem difficult to ignore ongoing gaps between self-perception and action. It's easier than you might think because we get so much help from others. We're all unconscious co-conspirators in an implied social contract to keep each other comfortably unaware of discrepancies.

Take a closer look in almost any meeting or encounter and it's right before your eyes. In the following example, watch Susan, a cubicle-dwelling supervisor in an insurance company, meet with Dale, one of her subordinates. Dale has been griping that he's underpaid and overqualified for his mail clerk job. He constantly reminds everyone that he is far too good for his current post because he is a bona fide *college graduate*. Susan summons Dale to offer him a new position as an underwriting trainee. Pay careful attention to what Susan and Dale say to each other. You'll also be privy to what Susan was thinking and feeling, but *not* saying, during the meeting.

Susan's Underlying Thoughts	***What Susan and Dale Said***
	SUSAN: We're creating a new trainee position and want to offer it to you. The job will carry a salary increase, but let me tell you something about the job first.
I wonder if his education makes him feel that society owes him a living without any relationship to his abilities or productivity.	DALE: O.K. But the salary increase has to be substantial so I can improve my standard of living. I can't afford a car. I can't even afford to go out on a date.
	SUSAN: You'll start as a trainee working with an experienced underwriter.

It's important work, because selecting the right risks is critical to our results. You'll deal directly with our agents. How you handle them affects their willingness to place their business with us.

DALE: I'm highly educated. I can do anything I set my mind to. I could do the job of a supervisor right now. I don't see how risk selection is that difficult.

How can he be so opinionated when he doesn't know anything about underwriting? How's he going to come across to the people he'll have to work with? The job requires judgment and willingness to listen.

SUSAN: Dale, we believe you're highly intelligent. You'll find you can learn many new skills working with an experienced underwriter. I'm sure many of the things you know today came from talented professors and teachers. Remember, one of the key elements in this job is your willingness to work closely with other people, and to listen to their opinions.

That's the first positive response I've heard.	DALE: I'm looking for something that will move me ahead. I'd like to move into the new job as soon as possible.
	SUSAN: Our thought is to move you into this position immediately. We'll outline a training schedule for you. On-the-job and classroom, with testing at the end of each week.
We owe him a chance, but I doubt he'll succeed. He's got some basic problems.	DALE: Testing is no problem. I think you'll find I score extremely high in anything I do.

What's wrong with this picture? Plenty. Without knowing it, Susan and Dale are doing a superb job of keeping each other in the dark. Dale can't understand why no one recognizes his talents. But he has no clue that his actions continually backfire. He's one of those political victims discussed in Chapters 3 and 4: looking out for himself, but not doing a very good job of it. He wants to impress Susan, but his constant self-promotion reinforces his public persona as an opinionated, arrogant candidate for failure. But Dale doesn't know this, and Susan doesn't tell him. At the very moment Susan is worrying that Dale will offend coworkers by not listening to them, she tells him, "We think you're intelligent." Susan has good reason to doubt Dale's ability to listen, since he doesn't seem to hear her very well. If he can't listen to his boss, what's the chance he'll hear anyone else? Yet she leaves the meeting planning to move Dale into a new position while expecting that he'll fail. In fact, she colludes in the coming disaster by skirting the topic of Dale's self-defeating behavior. In protecting herself and Dale from a potentially uncomfortable encounter, Susan helps to ensure that no one learns anything. The blind lead the blind, and no one notices.

There's nothing special about the encounter between Susan and Dale. Similar things happen everywhere every day. The Dales of the world dig their way into deep holes. The Susans help them stay oblivious as they shovel. One management expert, Chris Argyris, calls it "skilled incompetence"—using well-practiced skills to produce the opposite of what you intend.* Dale wants Susan to appreciate his virtues. Instead, he strengthens her belief that he's arrogant and naive. Susan would like Dale to recognize his limitations, but unintentionally reassures him he's fine as is. It happens to all of us more than we realize. We don't walk our talk. Others notice the discrepancy, but don't tell us. We see cluelessness in everyone but in ourselves. As a result, effectiveness deteriorates and learning is rare—if it happens at all.

Years ago, Joe Luft and Harry Ingam developed a simple way to think about this issue: the Johari window. Their main idea: There are some things true about any of us that we know about, and others that we don't recognize. At the same time, there are things true about us that others know, and things that they don't. Putting those two dimensions together, you come up with a four-pane window, as shown in Figure 5-1.

*From an article in *Harvard Business Review,* September 1986, entitled "Skilled Incompetence."

Figure 5-1. Johari window.

	Known to Others	*Unknown to Others*
Known to Self	Public Self	Hidden Self
Unknown to Self	Blind Self	Uncharted Self

We'll tour the Johari window using a notorious example, the impeachment follies arising from President Bill Clinton's relationship with Monica Lewinsky. After the first "Monicagate" allegations surfaced, Clinton acknowledged only that he and Lewinsky knew each other casually. That much was public. But Clinton denied a sexual relationship with "that woman." He hoped to keep that hidden: known to him, but not to others. In the past, Clinton had successfully survived multiple "bimbo eruptions." This time, though, the camouflage had mixed results. It made it harder for the public to make sense out of a confusing mix of allegations and denials. But Clinton seemed blind to the fact that few people really bought his denials.

In trying to fathom the president's reckless, self-destructive actions, we find ourselves in the Johari window's bottom right pane. We're plumbing uncharted depths of Bill Clinton's character in search of what is likely as mysterious to him as to the rest of us. Clinton's prosecutors—Kenneth Starr and the impeachment "managers" from the House of Representatives—had their own problems with the Johari window. Passionately convinced of the justice of their cause, they could never understand why so much of the American public branded them as sanctimonious, politically motivated hypocrites.

When we're out of touch with how others see us, our actions misfire. But much of the time we don't know that we missed the target. Or, we know something went wrong, but don't know what. To learn about our blind spots, we need feedback from others. Similarly, others need our help to become aware of what they don't know about themselves. We have a choice to make. Are we willing to risk giving or getting feedback? We have at least three options: (1) keep muddling through; (2) exploit others' vulnerability; or (3) focus on learning. Let's explore the pluses and minuses of each.

FRANK 'N' HOPE: *IGNORANCE IS BLISS?*

Frank:	Anything come out of the workshop last week?
Hope:	Johari window.
Frank:	Some kind of Hindu philosophy?
Hope:	A way to think about what we know about ourselves and what others know about us. Most of the time we only deal with our public side.
Frank:	That's more than I want to know about most people.
Hope:	Another side is what I know about you that you don't know.
Frank:	You wish.
Hope:	I know. Want a sample?
Frank:	You've only seen what I want you to see. I keep everyone guessing.
Hope:	What if you're only fooling yourself?
Frank:	If I need a shrink, I'll tell you.

1. *Muddling through.* It's not the most exciting or heroic option, but plodding along a comfortable path is sometimes better than going crazy or sticking your neck out. Maybe you work in a place that instantly punishes anyone who does anything risky. Sometimes things are so hopeless that raising the dead would be easier than breathing life into our workplace. On the other hand, maybe the status quo isn't so bad. Muddling through may let you survive. Maybe you'll even be modestly productive, until a better day or a better job comes along.

2. *Exploit others' vulnerability.* You can look at others' blindness and vulnerability as an opportunity. It can be an opportunity to be helpful and supportive, or to make headway at others' expense. For example, subordinates usually know more about their bosses than bosses know about themselves. Unconsciously and automatically, we study people in power. Anticipating their moods, quirks, and needs is a survival skill. You can use your understanding of others' quirks to cover for them and keep them out of trouble. You can help them out in areas where you know they're at risk. It promotes teamwork, and makes you all the more valuable. On the other hand, you can also use other people's vulnerability to manipulate or undermine them. Scott Adams made this point in a cartoon in which Dilbert and Wally take boyish pleasure in realizing that they can get away with any insult to their boss, so long as they begin by saying, "With all due respect, sir. . . ." If you study the people around you carefully, you learn what image to project or button to push to get what you want or to induce them to self-destruct. It's a sneaky form of psychological jujitsu. Machiavelli understood this 500 years ago:

> It is not essential, then, that a Prince should have all the good qualities enumerated above, but it is most

> essential that he should *seem* to have them; I will even venture to affirm that if he has and invariably practices them all, they are hurtful, whereas the appearance of having them is useful. . . . A Prince should therefore be very careful that nothing ever escapes his lips which is not replete with the five qualities above named, so that to see and hear him, one would think him the embodiment of mercy, good faith, integrity, humanity, and religion. . . . Everyone sees what you seem, but few know what you are.*

Strategic hypocrisy. Powerful stuff. But dangerous. It's not so easy to *appear* to have good qualities if you really don't. Sooner or later, people will notice the gap. When they do, they get suspicious and look for ways to defend themselves. Not long ago, a manager told us about a former colleague, Stan. "Stan's the most manipulative guy I've ever known. Never gave a damn about anyone but himself. For a long time, it seemed like he could walk on water. But he made a *lot* of folks *really mad*. Eventually a few of us got up a little conspiracy. We made sure some stories about Stan got to the right people. Before he knew what hit him, he was out of a job. Can't say I care if he ever gets another one."

*Niccolò Machiavelli, *The Prince* (New York: Bantam Books, 1984), Chapter 18.

FRANK 'N' HOPE: *STAN'S DEMISE*

Frank:	I knew Stan. He never really got over losing his job.
Hope:	Maybe you and Stan have a lot in common. Both pols?
Frank:	I'm smarter than he was.
Hope:	Didn't Stan think he was pretty clever?
Frank:	Not after they took him down.
Hope:	Maybe there's some lessons here for you?
Frank:	Stan made two mistakes. He got caught. And he didn't jump in a foxhole when things got hot.
Hope:	You hear any hounds barking in the distance?

If you're politically astute and untroubled by selective manipulation, you may thrive on exploiting others' blindness. But, beware the risks. Sooner or later you might suffer a fate like poor Stan's.

3. *Focus on learning.* There's a third option. Learn. Maybe even help others learn. When you're well down the feeding chain, it's easy to figure that learning is someone else's job. That's a bad assumption for both you and your organization. Your present or future value to any workplace rests on your knowledge, skills, and motivation. If you keep learning, you can't lose.

No area of learning is more important than mastering your relationships with others. Even though we learn mostly from experience, we learn too little from our interpersonal encounters. Remember Susan and Dale. They met to talk about issues they both cared about. Yet neither got what he or she wanted, and no one learned anything. In a related example, a new boss held his first meeting with his staff. His goal was to energize and rally the troops. He opened with a critique of the group's past performance. The troops were energized, but not quite the way he had in mind. Everyone felt abused and enraged. Most of the talent started polishing resumes and looking for new jobs. The rest looked for ways to cover their rear ends. Of course, no one shared any of this with the boss. Over the next few months, he wondered why he was losing the good people and retaining mostly mediocre, risk-averse employees.

Knowing the link between actions and outcomes is basic to learning. We act, assess the outcomes, and then decide what to do next. The challenge in learning from relationships is that it's hard to know the results unless others tell us. They usually don't. Or they do it badly. But if you understand a few basic principles of interpersonal feedback, you can accelerate your own learning, and, maybe improve others' as well:

- *Ask and you shall receive.* People often withhold feedback because they're not sure you want it. Asking is the easiest way to get honest feedback. This takes persistence and skill in framing the right questions. But keep at it and you'll expand your learning opportunities. If you simply ask a friend or colleague, "What did you think about my report/speech/tie/dress/etc.," the first response you get will often amount to vague reassurance ("Seemed fine to me."). Not much help. Follow up with more specific probes: "What do you think worked best?" "What could I have done to make it better?" "What message do you think the audience took away?" People are reluctant to risk telling us more than we want to know. Persistence makes your requests clear and credible.

- *Say thank you.* The risk of asking for feedback is that you may not like what you hear. If that's true, say so, because the other will sense it. But be sure to thank anyone who tries to help. "Thanks. That's helpful, even if it isn't what I was hoping to hear." If you respond to a gift by rejecting it, criticizing it, or inducing guilt, the flow of future offerings evaporates very fast.
- *Ask before giving.* Feedback can do more harm than good. When someone doesn't want honest input, catching them off guard will breed suspicion and defense rather than receptivity and learning (Figure 5-2 gives an example). How do you know if feedback is welcome? Much of the time, people aren't expecting or even thinking about it. You can usually find out with a few simple questions. One gentle but reliable

Figure 5-2. Feedback has its risks.

approach is to ask how they felt about whatever they did: "How did you feel your presentation went?" "How are you feeling about your role on this team?" This kind of question gets others thinking. They may ask for your reactions, or, at least, give you an opening to ask whether they'd like to hear more. In any event, their response will help you assess whether they'll welcome your input.

- *When asked, give your best.* With or without prompting, people will sometimes solicit your reactions to something they did. Resist the temptation to offer reassuring platitudes. But brutal confrontation is even worse. You won't produce much learning with messages like, "That's the dumbest thing I've ever seen anyone do! How could you be so stupid?" Instead, describe as specifically as you can what you saw and how you reacted. It's not much help to tell someone, for example, "The whole presentation was a flop." A more specific version of the same message might be, "Your presentation made a number of interesting points, but after a while, I lost track and wasn't sure of your main message."
- *Tell the truth.* It's familiar advice that almost everyone endorses. And almost everyone violates. The primary culprit is fear. We'd say what we think if we weren't afraid of the consequences. Look at the following conversation between a boss and a subordinate. They're both about to be killed. Why? Two reasons. First, the boss has made a bad mistake, though he doesn't know it. Second, the subordinate is reluctant to tell the truth.

The boss is the captain of a DC-8 jet airplane. The subordinate is his copilot. They're flying an approach into the airport at Cold Bay, Alaska. The airport is surrounded by mountains, and there are only two safe routes in. Both pilots know this, and both are looking at the same approach chart. But the captain, who's flying, is off-track. Looking out the window won't help, because it's dark and they're in the clouds.

(At 5:36 A.M.)
CAPTAIN: Where's your DME? (*Translation: How far are we from the airport?)*
COPILOT: I don't have a reading. Last reading was 40 miles.
(At 5:37 A.M.)
COPILOT: Are you going to make a procedure turn?
CAPTAIN: No, I . . . I wasn't going to.
(Pause)
COPILOT: What kind of terrain are we flying over?
CAPTAIN: Mountains everywhere.
(Pause)
(At 5:39 A.M.)
COPILOT: We should be a little higher, shouldn't we?
CAPTAIN: No, 40 DME [40 miles from the airport], you're all right.
(At 5:40 A.M.)
CAPTAIN: I'll go up a little bit higher here. No reason to stay down that low so long.

(The captain climbed briefly to 4,000 feet, then started down again.)
(At 5:41 A.M.)
FIRST OFFICER: The altimeter is alive. (*Translation: We're very close to those mountains.)*

(At 5:42 A.M.)

FIRST OFFICER: Radio altimeters. Hey, John, we're off course! Four hundred feet from something!

Six seconds later the airplane was destroyed when it crashed into a mountain.

It's tempting to join the unconscious collusion to expand personal cluelessness. But think carefully about whether you want to join this conspiracy. You can avoid rocking the boat and muddle along with everyone else. If you're in a truly toxic workplace, that may be a safe and sane option, even though it mires you deeper in a rut. You could also follow Machiavelli's advice: Play it close to the vest and take advantage of others' blindness. Or you could set out on the high road of learning. The ability to learn from others and help them learn from you is rare. That alone makes it a distinctive and potent skill. Paraphrasing Robert Burns, "Oh what a gift the giver gives us, to see ourselves as others see us." So it is in our modern places of work.

ESCAPING CLUELESSNESS V: KNOWING OURSELVES

- WE ALL SUFFER FROM GAPS BETWEEN WHAT WE DO AND WHAT WE THINK WE'RE DOING.
- BETTER RELATIONSHIPS BEGIN WITH KNOWING OURSELVES.
- DECIDE WHETHER TO MUDDLE, EXPLOIT, OR LEARN.
- WE LEARN AND HELP OTHERS LEARN THROUGH INTERPERSONAL FEEDBACK.
  - YOU'LL GET FEEDBACK WHEN YOU ASK FOR IT.
  - SAY THANK YOU.
  - ASK BEFORE YOU OFFER.
  - WHEN ASKED, GIVE YOUR BEST.
  - TELL THE TRUTH.

6

Motivating, Empowering, and Teaming: Real Stuff or Fool's Gold?

When employees are treated like commodities, they're not likely to treat customers like royalty. Most of us get angry when we're ignored, exploited, mistreated, or manipulated. When we're angry, we're tempted to get even. A better option is to improve the job we have, or find a better one.

In 1998, Rtmark, an anticorporate association based in California, urged workers to set aside the first Monday in April to phone in sick. The rationale was that "the capitalist world treats humans as machines, so why shouldn't we treat them as machines too?" For those who felt calling in sick was too risky, Rtmark suggested that they "make the most of the day by sabotaging their job from within." Suggestions for sabotage included ordering the boss subscriptions to munitions magazines and "speaking in a bad English accent all day."*

*S. Lyall, "Shirkers Unite! Tomorrow Is Your Day," *The New York Times,* April 5, 1998, p. BU-9.

Rtmark extends an ancient tradition. Aversion to work is a very old sentiment. More than 2,000 years ago, the author of Ecclesiastes wrote, "What do mortals get from all the toil and strain with which they labor under the sun? For all their days are full of pain, and their work is a vexation."* Assessments of work haven't improved much since. We talk about it as drudgery, a grind, the rat race. Work is what we have to do when we'd really rather be doing something else. It's why we hate Mondays and thank God for Fridays. Mark Twain's comment was typically pithy: "I do not like work, even when someone else does it." Danny McGoorty's sentiments were in the same vein: "I've never liked working. To me, a job is an invasion of privacy."

FRANK 'N' HOPE: *CAN WORK WORK?*

Frank:	Face it. Work sucks! You're lucky to survive one day at a time.
Hope:	You'd be surprised what we could do to make this place better.
Frank:	I'm surprised you're still so naive. This quality of work garbage is just a way to get more work for less money.
Hope:	But if it really gets to be a better place to work . . . ?
Frank:	You must still believe in the tooth fairy.

But there's another side. Twain was a tireless worker, an energetic and productive writer and lecturer who loved what

*Ecclesiastes 2:21–22, in the *Holy Bible: New Revised Standard Version* (Oxford: Oxford University Press, 1989).

he did, even if he hated to admit it. Noel Coward went so far as to say work was more fun than fun. Rudyard Kipling was typically exuberant:

> *And only the Master shall praise us, and only the Master shall blame.*
> *And no one shall work for money, and no one shall work for fame.*
> *But each for the joy of the working, and each, in his separate star,*
> *Shall draw the Thing as he sees It for the God of Things as They are.*

At its best, work offers challenge, creativity, achievement, contribution, and excitement. It's an expression of who we are. It's a big part of what we do and how we contribute to the world we live in. In Kahlil Gibran's words, "Work is love made visible."

Think about what work means to you and those you work with. Pain or pleasure? Draining or invigorating? Something to avoid or welcome? How well does your current situation measure up? If you don't like things as they are, what can you do? Maybe more than you think. There's a lot that you can do individually and with help from your friends to make work more rewarding and fulfilling.

In the first place, it helps to pick a good place to work. Organizations vary enormously in how well they treat people. Some make work exciting, rewarding, even fun. They get on *Fortune's* annual list of the 100 best companies to work for. Some employees *enjoy* going to work in the morning. You could be among them. Even if your current setting makes another list, falling somewhere between sweatshop and penal colony (like the employer in Figure 6-1), don't

Figure 6-1. One clue to look elsewhere for a job.

assume you're stuck in perpetual purgatory. Look for better options. Either improve your current situation, or find one that suits you better.

How do you sniff out a good workplace? When you're on a job interview, spend as much time studying the place as you do trying to impress people. We'll give you a checklist of what to look for. There's a set of values, beliefs, and practices that good employers use to make work less dispiriting and more fulfilling. These progressive approaches have been proven over time; they're well known and widely publicized. You might think they would be in wider use. Unfortunately, most workplaces still give them only lip service.

Good employers embrace a pair of simple ideas:

1. A better workforce generally produces better work.
2. The best way to get and keep a talented workforce is to treat people well.

So progressive companies invest in people. To get a good return on investment, they make sure employees have the space and resources to use their knowledge and skills.

This isn't rocket science. But it's easier to say than do; it takes commitment and persistence. Many companies promise. Few deliver. Too many inadvertently follow Dogbert's advice: They pretend to care. We noted in Chapter 5 that there's a lot of slippage between what people say and do. It's the same with organizations. Companies often say the right words: "We put our people first." "People are our most important asset." But when the going gets tough, the bottom line prevails, and employees finish last. Executive payouts soar even as layoffs escalate. Average total compensation for chief executives of big U.S. companies increased 35 percent in 1997, and 36 percent in 1998 to stand at a cool $10.6 million. That was more than 400 times the pay of the average factory worker, whose annual take-home came in at a little over $25,000 after a lavish raise of almost $700.* With the big boss earning more in a day than blue-collar workers make in a year, it's small wonder that waves of disappointment and cynicism roll across the corporate landscape. It's why millions of workers look to Dilbert as a comforting island of truth in a swirling sea of hypocrisy.

Still, there are many places that do it right. They're not perfect, but far better than most. That's usually good enough that the organization and its workforce both come out ahead. The company prospers because it has a more talented, motivated, loyal, and free-spirited team than its opponents. Workers win because work is more fun and more rewarding. That's a mutually potent edge—in sports, in business, or anywhere else.

If it's that simple, why don't more companies do it? One impediment is simple, short-term thinking of the kind

*From "Executive Pay," *Business Week,* April 20, 1998, pp. 64–65; April 19, 1999, pp. 72–90.

we discussed in Chapter 2. Investing in people is a long-term wager. You spend now in hopes of a payoff later on. That's tough to do if it's hard to see beyond next week's numbers. Take training as an example. If you send someone off to a course or a workshop, the bill comes right away. The benefits are more elusive and take longer to materialize. If you're under the gun to hit the numbers this month or quarter, the training budget almost screams, "Cut me!" Only a long-term commitment to building an able, committed workforce will stave off the urge to whack training first.

HOW THE BEST PLACES INVEST IN PEOPLE

Good places to work generally use five strategies to invest in their workforce. Check out how your employer stacks up against these criteria.

1. *Hire the right people and reward them well.* Companies that know what kind of people they want do what it takes to get them. Southwest Airlines looks for people with an attitude and sense of humor. Microsoft goes after the world's smartest and toughest nerds. Both build hiring and reward practices to achieve their goals. In hiring interviews, Southwest tests applicants' sense of humor. Microsoft challenges candidates to solve devilishly tough brainteasers.

Once they hire the right people, good employers do all they can to keep them. They pay well and offer a strong benefits package. How can they afford this? Because it gets them better, more loyal and more productive people. Smart companies understand that paying people less actually costs more if it leads to high turnover, low productivity, poor service, and lousy quality.★

The best employers also provide options such as flex-time and child care that keep people sane while they're being productive. They create ways to share the wealth and give workers a piece of the action. Microsoft has transformed so many employees into millionaires that many of the best and brightest flock there for a piece of the action. (Bill Gates's $500,000 annual salary in 1997 made him arguably America's most underpaid CEO, although his $40 to $50 billion stake in his company probably provided a measure of financial security.†) When organizations shower benefits on a few top executives while stiffing everyone else, they send a clear message that the troops don't count.

2. *Protect jobs and promote from within.* You also build loyalty by promoting from within and providing high levels of job security. Good companies don't crank out pink slips at the first sign of a business downturn. They look for creative ways to redeploy people. Layoffs are the last, not the first, thing they do. If your company is loyal to you, you're a lot more likely to return the favor. Loyalty means less turnover, which produces big long-term benefits. People who leave walk away with knowledge, experience, and, often, customers. A lot of business disasters have been traced to inexperi-

★The idea that more loyal and productive people are worth more is discussed in Edward A. Lawler's book, *From the Ground Up: Six Principles for Building the New Logic Corporation,* San Francisco: Jossey-Bass, 1996, and Jeffrey Pfeffer's "Six Dangerous Myths About Pay," *Harvard Business Review,* May-June 1998, pp. 108–119.

†Gates's pay package grew to $1.6 million in 1998, still low by CEO standards. Meanwhile, his wealth grew exponentially, from around $7 billion in 1992 to more than $75 billion by early 1999, on the strength of Microsoft's soaring stock. This made him the richest person in history, with about as much wealth as the poorer half of the U.S. population. See Andy Serwer's article, "How Bill Gates Invests His Money," in *Fortune,* March 15, 1999, pp. 68–71.

enced, short-term employees who antagonized customers, screwed up the product, or, literally, blew up the plant. With employees, as with customers, it's generally easier and cheaper to keep the ones you have than to recruit and train new hires. One of the most visible examples of this philosophy is Lincoln Electric, the world's largest manufacturer of arc welding equipment. In 1914 Lincoln established a policy that no employee with more than three years of service would be laid off. In the 1980s the company experienced a 40 percent year-to-year drop in demand for its products. Instead of shedding people, Lincoln converted production workers into sales representatives. They canvassed businesses rarely reached by the company's regular distribution channels. "Not only did these people sell arc welding equipment in new places to new users, but since much of the profit of this equipment comes from the sale of replacement parts, Lincoln subsequently enjoyed greater market penetration and greater sales as a consequence." Facing similar circumstances, Japan's Mazda had similar results: "At the end of the year, when awards were presented to the best salespeople, the company discovered that the top ten were all former factory workers. They could explain the product effectively, and when business picked up, the fact that factory workers had experience talking to customers yielded useful ideas about product characteristics."*

3. *Invest in learning.* Good workplaces invest in learning, on-the-job as well as in workshops, courses, and seminars. Good hiring is a first step in building a top-notch workforce, but people rarely arrive at work with all the skills they need,

*Both of these quotations appear on page 47 of Jeffrey Pfeffer's book *Competitive Advantage Through People: Unleashing the Power of the Work Force* (Boston: Harvard Business School Press, 1994).

and they fall behind if they don't continue to upgrade. Building employees' skills and knowledge is an ongoing effort. Companies that do it well typically use several strategies:

- They make employee development and learning part of managers' job descriptions and hold them accountable for results.
- They provide a range of educational offerings—everything from short-term sessions on specific job skills to seminars and workshops on longer-range competencies.
- They systematically move people through a variety of experiences and assignments to broaden their skills and perspectives.
- They provide financial support to encourage employees to sign up for courses and degree programs away from work.

If all of the foregoing sounds like a fairy tale, totally unrelated to your work experience, it's a safe bet your current workplace is behind the learning curve. That's a bad sign—for you, and for the long-term prospects of your organization.

4. *Empower—give people information and room to run.* Investing in employees builds loyalty, skill, and motivation. It's a necessary first step. But if you treat people like serfs and micromanage the talent you've nurtured, you squander the returns on investment. Smart companies know that you have to empower as well as invest. People with brains want to think. People with talent want to use it. A team of superstars can't do much if its creative talents are shackled.

The basic idea of empowerment is so simple even a child can understand it. Doing it well is another matter. The first key is providing people with the information and resources they need to make and implement sensible decisions—simple things like sharing key financial indicators so workers can track how well the firm is doing. That lets them see firsthand how their efforts link to the bottom line. The pointy-haired bosses of the world are too scared to give people information or room to run. So they micromanage, tenaciously hoarding information and resources. They practice "mushroom management"—keep them in the dark, feed them manure, and wait for them to grow. They handcuff people and then complain about lack of initiative. They treat employees like children and wonder why they don't act like adults.

Information and resources provide basic tools people need. Autonomy and participation give them a chance to use what they have. Involving people in key decisions increases the likelihood that decisions will be right, well understood, and widely supported when they're implemented. When people have room to contribute their knowledge and skills, they often figure out better, more interesting, ways to be productive. Motivation dries up fast if your boss practices "snooper vision," constantly looking over your shoulder and barking orders.

5. *Promote diversity.* Good companies work at treating everyone well—workers as well as executives, women as well as men, Asians, Blacks, and Hispanics as well as whites, gays as well as straights. Sometimes they do it because they just think it's right. Often they do it because bad publicity, lawsuits, or government pressure forced them to. In 1994, Denny's Restaurants suffered a PR disaster and paid $54 million to settle discrimination lawsuits. The bill was even higher for Shoney's—$134 million. Both restaurant chains got religion as a result. So did Texaco, after the company's

stock market value dropped by half a billion dollars in the wake of a controversy over racism at the top.*

But mostly companies promote diversity because it makes business sense. These days, affirmative action is a political football in Washington much more than in executive suites. More than half the U.S. workforce is female, and about a fourth is Asian, Black, or Hispanic. It's tough to build a workforce if your business practices write off a majority of your potential talent. Plus, if you write off certain groups as employees, the word tends to get out, costing you customers as well.

Promoting diversity comes down to focus and persistence. Companies first have to decide to take it seriously. Then they build it into day-to-day management. They tailor recruiting practices to diversify the candidate pool. They have a variety of internal initiatives to help different people get ahead. They tie executives' bonuses to success in building a more diverse workforce. They work hard at eliminating glass ceilings. They work for a rich mix in their boards of directors. It takes more than lip service, and it won't happen overnight. A lot of companies still don't get it. But many that would have had trouble spelling the word diversity a decade or so ago have made impressive strides since.

SUMMING UP

Make notes in the table on the next page on how your company stacks up against the best of breed. If you find you're already at one of the best, congratulations! If not, stay tuned. Coming up next are ideas about how to make things better.

*For details, see G. Colvin, "The 50 Best Companies for Asians, Blacks, and Hispanics," *Fortune*, July 19, 1999, pp. 53–58.

What Good Companies Do	*What Your Company Does*
Hire the right people	
Keep them (promote from within, protect jobs, reward them well, give them a piece of the action)	
Invest in them (training, opportunities for growth and development)	
Empower them (provide information and support, autonomy, opportunities to make a difference)	
Promote diversity	

FRANK 'N' HOPE: *WORLD'S WORST?*

Frank: Someone should make a list of the world's worst places to work. We'd be right up there.

Hope: That could change.

Frank: Not in my lifetime.

Hope: Do you like how things are?

Frank: What's the difference? Happiness doesn't pay the bills.

THE SLAVE GALLEY—FIX IT OR LEAVE IT!

You may be wondering if your chance to apply these great ideas about quality of work will only come when you're hired to run General Electric. Meanwhile, what do you do if your cubicle is cramped, your boss is an ogre, and your workplace feels like a slave galley (see Figure 6-2)? Recall a key piece of political advice: No matter where you are, you always have options. You're powerless only as long as you

Figure 6-2. A slave galley by another name is still a lousy place to work.

"Human Resources."

think you are. You've got at least four routes to a better workplace: (1) Create your own do-it-yourself improvement program; (2) band together with some of your coworkers; (3) fight back; or (4) if all else fails and your workplace remains hopelessly toxic, leave and find another.

1. *Do-it-yourself improvement.* You improve things on your own by seeking out chances to contribute, learn, and have fun. Most workplaces have more things to be done than people to do them. Look for opportunities, and grab the attractive ones. Consider the following possibilities:

- Look for things beyond the routine. Find tasks that take you outside your usual responsibilities, and provide exposures to new places and people. Ask your boss what else you could do to help.
- Suggest a project that needs to be done. Maybe one where everyone is waiting for someone else to take the initiative.
- Pounce on any chances to learn that come your way. If you're eligible for educational benefits, be greedy; exploit them to the max. Sign up for any training opportunities that come along. Some may be hokey or worse, but most will have their share of learning nuggets.

2. *Form a personal growth coalition.* A do-it-yourself program can be even more effective if you recruit some coworkers to join you. Create a positive learning conspiracy. Talk about the best and worst features of your jobs. Brainstorm ways to make work more rewarding and fun. You'll probably find some things you can do as a team. Others may take buy-in or more budget from management. If so, make your case.

Some managers may be defensive about new twists they didn't think of themselves. But many will be receptive if you can explain the merits of your idea. There's plenty of evidence that both the company and employees benefit when work becomes more rewarding and fun.

3. *Fight back.* If your job is hellish and your boss abusive, it's tempting to follow the old advice, "Don't get mad, get even." Before going that way, keep in mind the personal risks are high. You're likely to infuriate bosses and may wind up in a shootout with a posse of the company's hired guns (often armed with law degrees). You may be branded as a traitor or saboteur. Old friends may give you a cold shoulder, and it can get very hard to find another job.

There's more than one way to fight back. Some ways are nothing more than mean-spirited expressions of personal pique—things like deliberately turning out crappy products, or spreading false rumors about the boss, or spiking the office coffee pot with urine (weird as it sounds, it's been done). Don't go there unless you think "suicide bomber" is a neat career opportunity. It's not very hard to do a lot of damage, but you're likely to hurt yourself as much as anyone else.

A second variety of fighting back is *getting even.* The idea was captured in a manuscript with the provocative title, "Employee Theft as a Form of Job Enrichment." Theft is one of a number of things employees do to even the accounts: "They screw us, why shouldn't we screw them a little in return." If the pay is lousy, the hours ridiculous, and the boss demonic, pilfering some of the merchandise is one way to enrich your job and improve your compensation package. Other ways to even the score include loafing, slowdowns, and, lately, surfing the Net on company time. These strategies generally have to stay hidden—you're in trouble if you get caught. For some workers, that's part of the thrill—

the satisfaction of successfully outwitting arrogant or clueless managers. But getting even doesn't do much to improve the conditions that make the job suck. Things just go further downhill in a spiral of mistrust, conflict, and inefficiency. The end, all too often, is that the plant closes or the company goes under because management and workers are busy fighting each other instead of producing what customers want.

There's still a third important category of fighting back: principled resistance to employer malfeasance. One common form is whistle-blowing: going public with allegations that your company is engaging in dangerous, unethical, or illegal practices. Some whistle-blowers try to operate anonymously via an unsigned letter or broadside, or by leaking documents. That sometimes works, but it tends to weaken the case. People are more suspicious when they don't know the source of allegations. Anonymous whistle-blowing is particularly infuriating to its targets, who generally see their antagonist as a coward and a traitor. When management really gets its back up, it typically does everything possible to identify the culprit. Woe be unto you if you're caught.

Public whistle-blowing is only for those with courage and stamina. As we noted in Chapter 3, you may be a hero to the public, but chances are good your employer will fire you, sue you for defamation, and blame you for any wrongdoing that's discovered. That's exactly what happened to an engineer who told the FBI that his company was falsifying test data on brakes for an Air Force fighter jet. And to an executive at a big agribusiness firm who reported that his employer was engaged in illegal price-fixing. Whistle-blowing has an honorable tradition, and in some cases is the only way to compel rogue employers to correct their illegitimate ways. It can be an act of genuine courage and leadership. But think carefully before taking the plunge. Make sure your case is strong. Even more important, make sure you're willing to pay the personal costs. They may be a lot higher than you think.*

4. *Find a better place to work.* If all else fails, maybe it's time to look elsewhere. Life is short, and work fills a lot of it. Don't let inertia, fear of change, or a paycheck chain you to a losing situation. You deserve a good job. Bad employers deserve to lose good people. If enough talent heads for the exit, employers sometimes get the message. In leaving, you might do everyone a favor.

Above all, find ways to have fun. There's no evidence that people produce more when they hate work. Even so, many workplaces seem determined to stamp out anything resembling pleasure. Ignore anyone who says you're paid to be miserable or that having fun at work is tantamount to ripping off the company. The human instinct for play and pleasure is remarkably resilient. So follow your basic instincts and go for it. Just keep in mind the difference between pleasure in work and the joys of sabotage or revenge. When you look for ways to add a little zest, fun, or humor to your work, you'll be amazed at the opportunities that show up. For example, there are the Southwest Airlines flight attendants who lace preflight safety announcements with large doses of stand-up comedy. It's more fun for employees, and more likely to get passengers' attention than the usual formulaic safety drone. Or the young worker at a tool and die company whose design for a new riveting machine made it almost as much fun as a video game: "It got to be like a game. Could you load the rivets fast enough to keep up with the machine? Eventually I had to speed the machine up, because the operators were beating it too much."

*If you're contemplating whistle-blowing, check out a very informative online guide at http://www.reporter.org/hillman/courage/index.html.

ESCAPING CLUELESSNESS VI: MAKING OR FINDING A BETTER JOB

- WORK DOESN'T HAVE TO BE MISERABLE.
- GOOD WORKPLACES
  - HIRE AND RETAIN THE RIGHT PEOPLE.
  - INVEST IN AND EMPOWER THEIR WORKFORCE.
- FIX YOUR JOB—OR GET A NEW ONE
  - FIX IT YOURSELF.
  - FORM A COALITION.
  - FIGHT BACK.
  - FIND A BETTER JOB.

Looking Ahead

- Intense competition pushes organizations to make the mistake of going for lean and mean, investing as little as possible in workers.
- To win in a global marketplace, organizations will have to attract and retain a motivated, educated workforce by:
  —Offering good pay and benefits
  —Investing in learning
  —Empowering
- People will continue to demand better working conditions. You should too.

SUGGESTIONS FOR FURTHER READING

The 100 Best Companies to Work for in America, by R. Levering and M. Moskowitz, is a good starting point for finding a better place to work. Another good source is *Fortune* magazine's annual list of the 100 best places to work in the United States. Daniel S. Levine's *Disgruntled: The Darker Side of the World of Work* is a compendium of horror stores from the workplace, along with an extensive discussion of strategies for fighting back. Levine maintains a website at *http://www.disgruntled.com*. In *The Joy of Work: Dilbert's Guide to Finding Happiness at the Expense of Your Co-Workers*, Scott Adams provides reams of advice for having more fun at work, but it's doubtful that he expects any sensible person to take his suggestions seriously.

See the Bibliography for publication details of these books.

PART IV

THE JOY OF BUREAUCRACY

Making Structure Work

7

MAPPING THE PECKING ORDER: THE PERENNIAL HIERARCHY

Have you ever felt like an oppressed serf on a medieval manor? Have you asked yourself why top management seems so distant and inaccessible? Or why middle managers make senseless decisions? Have you seen a coworker get promoted to management and change overnight into a bossy know-it-all? Have you ever moved from a technical to a managerial position and felt caught in the middle? All this and more flows from the pecking order you find in every workplace. Understanding how the hierarchy works helps to escape from mindless bureaucracy, rules, and red tape.

Modern organizations often resemble feudal hierarchies (see Figure 7-1). At the top is a monarch who more or less reigns over everything. Of course, the title today is dressed up with contemporary lingo. In business, monarchs are called chief executives, presidents, and managing directors. In government they carry titles such as president, governor, minister, or cabinet secretary. Schools and colleges have

Figure 7-1. Modern feudalism.

Reprinted with special permission of King Features Syndicate.

presidents, school superintendents, headmasters, and principals. Whatever their labels, monarchs preside over a corporate "kingdom." Their subjects often presume that the wisdom or folly of the monarch's rule is fateful for the realm's health and well-being. Monarchs' images are larger-than-life and closely identified with their domain. Microsoft is Bill Gates and vice versa. Few of Microsoft's millions of customers could identify anyone else who works for the company. Equating an organization with the current monarch puts a face on a large, impersonal entity. A monarch is also a convenient target for praise or blame. Everything we like or hate about Microsoft, its products, or its dominant position in the digital revolution, we lay at Bill Gates's doorstep.

What is less often noticed is that the office of the monarch is not a solo operation. There's a powerful inner circle, a palace guard—with titles like chief of staff, vice-president, assistant, or counsel. The inner circle is often invisible, operating behind the scenes. But it's formidable because it controls the flow of information in and out of the palace, and often acts in the name of the monarch.

Beyond the palace, scattered across the hinterland, are the lords. Like monarchs, lords govern their particular domains. But they report to the monarch or to another lord and serve more or less at their master's pleasure. Greater and lesser nobles (dukes, earls, viscounts, etc.) are still with us. But now we call them middle managers.

At the other end of the pecking order are the serfs: folks who do the basic work. In feudal times, serfs grew crops and plied trades. Later, the industrial revolution turned them into blue-collar workers. In recent years, the information economy has replaced production workers with Dilberts: legions of cubicle dwellers who stoke organizations' information furnaces. The new serfdom includes engineers, technicians, accountants, clerical staff, telemarketers, and a variety of other white-collar jobs. The common link: They're all "individual contributors," parked near the bottom of the hierarchy. They reign over no significant domain except their own small work space.

FRANK 'N' HOPE: *CAUGHT IN THE MIDDLE*

Frank:	The boss is always on my back to get more work out of my unit. Try getting blood from a turnip.
Hope:	Maybe you should stop squeezing?
Frank:	Easy to say if they're not running you through a ringer.
Hope:	Think you're alone? Face it, Frank, you're caught in the middle.
Frank:	I thought it would be easier when I got promoted. It's worse.
Hope:	Remember Robin Hood?
Frank:	Stole from the rich and gave to the poor?
Hope:	No. Built a high-performing team, and found ways to work around the system.

Barry Oshry* has spent his professional life studying the relationships among monarchs, lords, and serfs. He's found that the three groups live in distinct yet predictable worlds. Put someone in any of the three echelons. Soon his or her thoughts, feelings, and actions conform to the rules of that tier. Life at the top is similar across organizations and sectors. The same is true for the middle and bottom. Despite the rosy stereotypes, life at the top isn't easy. Elites live in a world of complexity, accountability, and burden. They're bombarded with information, questions, and problems, most of which are ambiguous and confusing. There's too much irrelevant information, and not nearly enough news they really need.

At the top, you're overwhelmed with too much to do and too little time and energy to get to it all. You feel responsible for the realm's overall health and performance. You're expected to chart a clear long-term course, make crisp decisions, and solve immediate problems. The stakes are very high. If you fall short or fail, you're afraid that war, famine, and pestilence will infect the entire domain. Still, there's no way you can do it all. But you're reluctant to delegate, because you're not sure your palace guard or lords can handle things. The burden of details and problems grows heavier and heavier. You age quickly, and fret over burnout, illness, or early death. Meanwhile, urgent problems keep piling up. Everything's falling apart and everyone's looking to you for answers. Your retainers don't want to move without your guidance. If they act, they're afraid you'll have their heads. Yet if they hesitate, they expect to be lacerated for indolence and sloth.

Jimmy Carter was a do-it-himself monarch, and his

*Author of *Seeing Systems: Unlocking the Mysteries of Organizational Life* (San Francisco: Berrett-Koehler, 1995).

presidency became a painful, downhill spiral. Ronald Reagan was different. At a European summit meeting, it became obvious that the president hadn't read his briefing book. When James Baker, the president's aide, pulled him aside to ask why, Reagan responded genially, "Well, Jim, *The Sound of Music* was on TV last night." Carter knew more about the details. But Reagan got reelected.

Monarchs like Reagan avoid much of the awesome responsibility of their role. They have more fun and feel less burdened because they cut their retainers a lot of slack. The palace guard and lords are delighted with the freedom to deal with their respective problems and priorities. Lax oversight lets them compete intensely for the monarch's favor and largesse, even though they're supposed to be team players. Their autonomy also frees them to go off in a variety of directions—some potentially dangerous. The Reagan presidency's most damaging episode originated within the White House itself. The Iran-Contra affair was a tale of clandestine arms sales to Iran with proceeds illegally diverted to Nicaraguan *contras*. All this was spearheaded by Colonel Oliver North and his colleagues in the National Security Council. Faced with a damning report from a commission he'd appointed, Reagan took refuge in a plea of ignorance. He acknowledged that "mistakes had been made," while claiming to be oblivious to his palace guard's actions. Only history will tell whether it got him off the hook.

When the prince and the pauper traded places in Mark Twain's famous novel, each was stunned at how the other lived. It's the same in most organizations. At the bottom of the food chain, serfs live a life very different from monarchs (see Figure 7-2). They're not weighed down by an endless burden of problems and responsibilities. They don't lie awake at night worrying about high-stakes decisions and un-

Figure 7-2. White-collar serfs.

finished tasks. In fact, their life is pretty simple: Show up, do a passable job, and go home. What's tough for them to understand is why upper management keeps screwing things up. They accuse bosses of micromanaging, giving silly orders, making bonehead decisions, and constantly changing course for no apparent reason. The serfs' biggest problem isn't complexity or responsibility. It's feeling vulnerable and helpless. "Bosses" make all the key decisions: how much serfs are paid, what they do, and whether they keep their jobs. Serfs feel manipulated, exploited, and underrewarded. They often compensate by tuning off or dropping out. In today's high-tech workplace, they build a virtual moat around their cubicle and surf the Internet. They often shun responsibility for workplace health or productivity. That's the bosses' jobs. In the same breath, they express doubts that their managers are smart enough to change lightbulbs.

Sandwiched between the monarch and serfs are the lords. Since they're dependent on the monarch, their well-being depends on faithfully executing directives from above. But the palace always seems to expect the impossible. It demands unrealistic levels of speed, efficiency, and productivity at very low cost. To deliver, lords need enthusiastic support from serfs, but eager serfs are hard to find. The monarch and palace guard wonder why the lords are so weak. Why can't they get anything done? Why can't they keep the serfs in line? Serfs are equally disappointed. Like Dilbert and his colleagues, they wonder why their bosses are such clueless, bumbling, petty tyrants. Why are decisions always late? Why do the lords constantly change their minds? Why can't they communicate better? Above all, why are wages and working conditions so dismal? Caught in the middle, lords struggle to satisfy both a demanding monarch and sullen serfs. Often they succeed in pleasing no one.

The struggle among monarchs, lords, and serfs has endured for centuries. It won't end soon. If you live in the modern equivalent of a feudal system, it helps to know your place in the pecking order and how it interacts with other levels. Your tier may be dreary, and the whole structure may be creaking. But there are three steps you can take to get a better read on your system and begin to move it in more productive directions.

1. *Study the formal system.* As we said in Chapter 2, simple thinking keeps you systems-blind. It's easy to find yourself imprisoned in a nonproductive hierarchy, wandering around a confusing labyrinth without a map. This aimless action breeds lots of logjams and accidents. It's painful personally, and doesn't do much for overall efficiency. Study the map in Figure 7-3, which shows some of the forces that produce the pattern of relationships among monarchs, lords, and serfs. It shows each level in the hierarchy responding in predictable ways to the pressures it experiences. The frustrating spiral will continue indefinitely unless participants in at least one tier of the hierarchy see what's happening and design alternative ways to respond.

Figure 7-3. Systems map: monarchs, lords, and serfs.

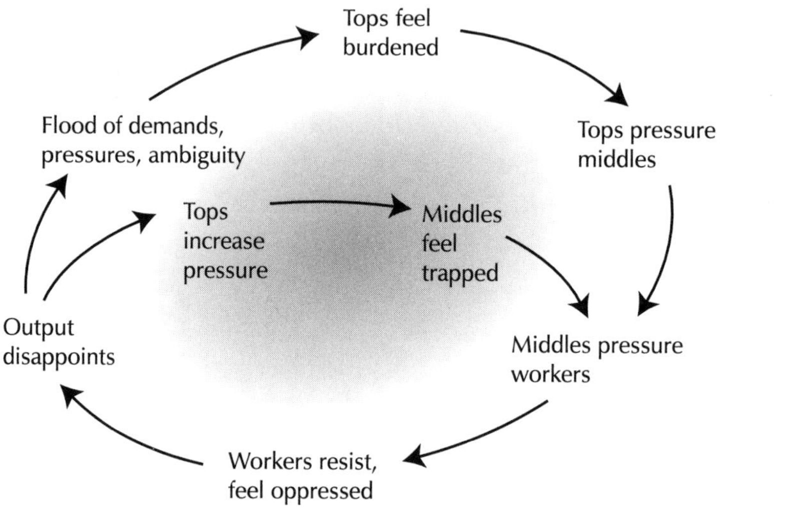

Understanding the enduring universal relationships among monarchs, lords, and serfs is a start. But you'll need to fit the map to your terrain by filling in local details. Think of yourself as a workplace Columbus or Magellan. Look for opportunities to move about and spend time at different levels of the system. Notice which people or groups seem to have a lot of clout, and which have none. Pinpoint those who are in the know and have access to key information, as well as those who are perpetually in the dark. Identify the people who are overburdened and those who are underworked. Who feels responsible for everything? Who feels responsible for nothing? Are some individuals or units isolated and disconnected while others feel squeezed and swamped? Mapping the maze will eventually let you spend less time wandering down blind alleys and butting your head against unanticipated obstacles. You're also likely to get a lot more done.

2. *Blame less and understand more.* It's more productive to understand what others are up against than to blame them for succumbing to problems and pressures in their positions. Regardless of politics or personality, it's easy to feel burdened if you're at the top, torn and ineffective if you're in the middle, and oppressed if you're at the bottom. Knowing your place helps you understand what's going on and why you feel as you do. But it also helps to know what other people are up against. We typically see only our own small piece of a much larger puzzle. We find it hard to understand where we fit in, much less what the whole hierarchy is all about. Oshry calls it "spatial blindness":

> *We see our part of the system*
> *but not the whole;*
> *we see what is happening with us*
> *but not what is happening elsewhere;*
> *we don't see what others' worlds are like, the issues they are dealing with,*
> *the stresses they are experiencing;*
> *we don't see how our world impacts theirs*
> *and how their world impacts ours;*
> *we don't see how all the parts influence one another**

Knowing another person's problems and pressures helps you deal with them more effectively. A friend of ours, Ellen, found herself in a new job where she needed the cooperation of all the senior executives. She spent her early weeks trying to get to know as much as possible about the monarch and palace guard. She quickly learned that none of her superiors

*Barry Oshry, *Seeing Systems: Unlocking the Mysteries of Organizational Life* (San Francisco: Berrett-Koehler, 1995), p. xii.

liked each other very much. Their prior efforts to cooperate spawned a continuing saga of disappointment and dismay. The good news was that she learned a lot about individuals' agenda, as well as some very helpful personal details. One of the senior managers was the local Rambo—invariably gruff and intimidating—unless you knew that he loved to talk football. Ellen wasn't much of a fan, but she became one for the purpose of building a relationship. A few minutes of gridiron chatter here and there did a lot to grease the wheels.

When we only know our role and don't understand what others are up against, it's easy to assume there's something wrong with them personally. Around the world, top echelons are disappointed with middle managers, wondering why they don't have more initiative, guts, and creativity. They ask why those in the middle are so defensive and resistant to change. The logical conclusion is that the middles need to be fixed. Maybe a good training program would light a fire under them. Or maybe they're just hiring errors who should be replaced with more talented new blood. But no amount of training or new blood makes much difference if the pyramid remains unchanged. That applies to all levels. Nothing will happen until monarchs, lords, and serfs change how they relate to one another. How? It's easy to say but hard to do.

3. *Step out of the flow or swim upstream.* The forces operating on monarchs, lords, and serfs are so reliable and powerful that it's easiest to just go with the flow. It feels safe, sound, and comfortable. But it keeps both you and the system stuck. The way out is to swim against the tide of expectations, or to step outside the flow. Step outside your role. Do something different and unexpected. If you're at the top, unburden yourself. Don't take responsibility for every problem someone throws your way. If you're in the middle, take initiative

and responsibility instead of waiting passively for direction for the top. If you're at the bottom, look for opportunities to contribute.

Even if others try to treat you like a vassal, you don't have to act like one. Suppose, for example, that your boss gives you an assignment that seems as unpleasant as it is useless. It's easy to slump into a serf-like role: dully doing what you've been told to do, or pretending to comply while doing as little as you can get away with. But there are other options. You could ask questions: What's the goal of this assignment? Why is it important? What priority should I give it compared to other things I'm working on? Such questions can get your boss thinking while gently communicating that you'd prefer to be treated as a colleague rather than a galley slave. A better understanding of the boss's rationale can also help you to suggest alternatives: ways to simplify or improve or expand the assignment to make it more valuable for you and the organization. So you could say: "If the goal is saving money, how about if we do it this way?" Or: "Before we start on this, should we check with marketing, or get data from engineering?" Or: "With this kind of problem, it usually works better if we. . . ." Whatever role you're in, look for creative alternatives to going with the flow. If it feels exciting and scary at the same time, you might be on the verge of something powerful and productive.

FROM MONARCHY TO BUREAUCRACY

Understanding the thinking and the dynamics of different structural strata—monarchs, lords, and serfs—helps you decipher one dimension of life at work. But modern organizations put a new spin on feudal life. In the old days, monarchs were born into the role and governed through royal fiat. Lords inherited their position through their bloodline, not their managerial talent. Even highly talented serfs were generally stuck in their role. In the new order, rationality has surpassed patrimony as the yardstick for sorting people into different organizational levels. It's called bureaucracy, a concept elaborated early in the twentieth century by Max Weber, a German sociologist.*

Weber saw the limits of a system based on birth rather than merit. He described an organizational form that was relatively new at the time. It assigned responsibilities and allocated authority based on efficiency, was governed by a clear, formal set of rules, and outlined technical qualifications for every position. Rules and standardization, rather than imperial dictate and whim, became the coin of the realm. Rules, policies, and standard operating procedures (SOPs) were put in place to help people work more efficiently. This helped everyone—monarchs, lords, and serfs—feel more secure. It also created coordination across different activities to ensure a well-integrated effort. If everyone conforms to the law of the land, things should get done more efficiently, unless the laws are outdated or misguided. A kingdom held together by predictable routine is reliable and predictable. But not always productive, particularly when exceptions and new problems come along. The following scenario is an example.†

Mr. Berman was a guest in a London hotel. He was a

*Max Weber, *Wirtschaft und Gesellschaft, 1922*. First published in English as *The Theory of Economic and Social Organization* (Talcott Parsons, translator) (New York: Free Press, 1947).

†This story can be found in a number of sites on the Internet, usually with an introduction stating that an unnamed hotel submitted it to London's *Sunday Times*. We think it's a true story, but we don't know its age, and have not been able to verify the original source. Even if it never happened, it could have. Sometimes fiction is truer than nonfiction. That might be the case here.

frequent traveler with well-seasoned ways. The problem was that his ways didn't align very well with the hotel's routines and procedures. He tried to communicate his concerns. What follows may not sound all that different from experiences you've had.

Dear Maid,

Please do not leave any more of those little bars of soap in my bathroom since I have brought my own bath-sized Dial.

Please remove the six unopened little bars from the shelf under the medicine chest and another three in the shower soap dish. They are in my way.

Thank you.

S. Berman

Dear Room 635,

I am not your regular maid. She will be back tomorrow, Thursday, from her day off. I took the three hotel soaps out of the shower soap dish as you requested.

The six bars on your shelf I took out of your way and put on top of the Kleenex dispenser in case you should change your mind. This leaves only the three bars I left today, in accordance with my instructions from the management to leave three soaps daily.

I hope this is satisfactory.

Kathy, Relief Maid

Dear Maid,

I hope you are my regular maid.

Apparently Kathy did not tell you about my note to her concerning the little bars of soap.

When I got back to my room this evening I found that you had added three little Camays to the shelf under my medicine cabinet. I am going to be here in the hotel for two weeks and have brought my own bath-sized Dial, so I won't need those six little Camays that are on the shelf. They are in my way when shaving, brushing teeth, etc. Please remove them.

S. Berman

Dear Mr. Berman,

My day off was last Wednesday so the relief maid left three hotel soaps, which we are instructed to do by management.

I took the six soaps that were in your way on the

shelf and put them in the soap dish where your Dial was. I put the Dial in the medicine cabinet for your convenience.

I didn't remove the three complimentary soaps which are always placed inside the medicine cabinet for all new check-ins and which you did not object to when you checked in last Monday. Please let me know if I can be of further assistance.

Your regular maid, Dotty

Dear Mr. Berman,

The assistant manager, Mr. Kensedder, informed me this A.M. that you called him last evening and said you were unhappy with your maid service. I have assigned a new girl to your room. I hope you will accept my apologies for the inconvenience. If you have any future complaints, please contact me so I can give them my personal attention. Call extension 1108 between 8 A.M. and 5 P.M. Thank you.

Elaine Carmen, Housekeeper

Dear Miss Carmen,

It is impossible to contact you by phone since I leave the hotel for business at 7:45 A.M. and don't get back until 6 or 6:30 P.M. That's the reason I called Mr.

Kensedder last night. You were already off duty. I only asked Mr. Kensedder if he could do anything about those little bars of soap. The new maid you assigned me must have thought I was a new check-in today, since she left another three bars of hotel soap in my medicine cabinet along with her regular delivery of three bars on the bathroom shelf. In just 5 days here, I have accumulated twenty-four little bars of soap. Why are you doing this to me?

S. Berman

Dear Mr. Berman,

Your maid, Kathy, has been instructed to stop delivering soap to your room and remove the extra soaps. If I can be of further assistance, please call extension 1108 between 8 A.M. and 6 P.M. Thank you.

Elaine Carmen, Housekeeper

Dear Mr. Kensedder,

My bath-size Dial is missing. Every bar of soap was taken from my room including my own bath-sized Dial. I came in late last night and had to call the bellhop to bring me four little Cashmere Bouquets.

S. Berman

Dear Mr. Berman,

I have informed our housekeeper, Elaine Carmen, of your soap problem. I cannot understand why there was no soap in your room since our maids are instructed to leave three bars of soap each time they service a room. The situation will be rectified immediately.

Please accept my apologies for the inconvenience.

Martin L. Kensedder, Assistant Manager

Dear Miss Carmen,

Who the hell left fifty-four little bars of Camay in my room? I came in last night and found fifty-four little bars of soap. I don't want fifty-four little bars of Camay. I want my one damn bar of bath-sized Dial. Do you realize I have fifty-four bars of soap in here? All I want is my bath-sized Dial. Please give me back my bath-sized Dial.

S. Berman

Dear Mr. Berman,

You complained of too much soap in your room, so I had them removed. Then you complained to Mr. Kensedder that all your soap was missing, so I personally returned them, the twenty-four Camays that had been taken and the three Camays you are supposed to receive daily. I don't know anything about the four Cashmere Bouquets.

Obviously your maid, Kathy, did not know I had returned your soaps so she also brought twenty-four Camays plus the three daily Camays.

I don't know where you got the idea that this hotel issues bath-sized Dial. I was able to locate some bath-sized Ivory, which I left in your room.

Elaine Carmen, Housekeeper

Dear Miss Carmen,

Please ask Kathy when she services my room to make sure the stacks of soap are neatly piled and dusted. Also, please advise her that stacks of more than four have a tendency to tip.

May I suggest that my bedroom window sill is not in use and will make an excellent spot for future soap deliveries. One more item: I have purchased another bar of bath-sized Dial, which I am keeping in the hotel vault in order to avoid further misunderstandings.

S. Berman

Clearly Berman's feelings about soap were unusually strong, but his initial request still seems straightforward. He wanted no soap other than the bar of Dial he brought with him. Sensibly enough, he left a note for the maid. Berman probably thought his message was crystal clear. Kathy, the relief maid, found it a bit more difficult to decode. The note said "remove from the shelf," but not "remove from the room." Trying her best to please her guest, Kathy relocated the soap, as per his instructions. Since she felt bound by official soap policy, she also left the customary three additional bars of Camay.

What happened here? The hotel rightfully had standard procedures to ensure that guests always had a plentiful supply of soap. The routines worked fine for most guests, but not for Berman. In his case, the programs ensured that Berman got lots of something he didn't want. Berman's notes continually puzzled the hotel staff. A "soap problem," in their experience, always meant a shortage, not a surplus.

When Dotty, the regular maid, received her first note from Berman, she was also confused. Rather than getting rid of the Camay on the shelf, she decided to move it to the soap dish, where his Dial was. Since she had to put the Dial somewhere, she moved it to the medicine cabinet "for your convenience." When Berman got back that evening, he was dumbfounded that the staff couldn't follow such simple instructions. No one from housekeeping was available at that hour, so he talked to the assistant manager, Mr. Kensedder. We don't know exactly what transpired in their conversation, but Kensedder followed the hotel's usual channels. He left a message for the housekeeper, Ms. Carmen, indicating that Berman was unhappy with his maid service. Carmen wasn't sure what the problem was, but assigned another maid. Trying to go the extra mile, she also sent Berman a note encouraging him to phone her anytime between 8 and 5. If Berman and Carmen had ever talked, they might have resolved the issue. But Berman's schedule didn't permit it. Thus, the catastrophe continued to grow.

What we see is a fairly typical scenario. The SOPs are essential in many workplaces. They ensure efficient, reliable handling of routine, well-understood problems. Something as simple and stable as regular soap delivery fits the category nicely. But SOPs often choke on the unexpected and the nonroutine. The soap scenario features lots of one-way, top-down communication: Kensedder left messages for Carmen, and Carmen gave instructions to the maids. But two-way communication was almost nonexistent. As is customary in rule-bound, top-down structures, hotel staff industriously stuck to the rules in their job descriptions. Their notes to Berman were studiously polite and continually expressed a wish to serve him better. No one quite recognized that "doing their job" kept making things worse. Berman finally caught on. Recognizing at last that the hotel was determined to flood him with Camay, he capitulated, and asked only that it be neatly stacked and dusted.

FRANK 'N' HOPE: *IF THE SHIP SINKS, WHO GETS THE LIFEBOAT?*

Hope:	We need to stop fighting and start paying more attention to customers.
Frank:	That's management's job.
Hope:	No one will have a job if we go under.
Frank:	This place has been here a long time. It'll last till I retire.
Hope:	Unsinkable, huh? Like the *Titanic*.
Frank:	If we downsize, I figure it'll be women and children first.
Hope:	What if it's dump the deadwood?
Frank:	Too innovative. Management will never buy it.

Similar situations occur all the time in workplaces. Pyramids and standardization are often efficient, but they also have unintended side effects. The London hotel employees wanted to do a good job, but their efforts kept making things worse. It was almost as frustrating for them as for Berman. The question is, how can we avoid such unproductive spirals?

One of the more obvious possibilities is to focus everyone's attention on the customer or client. In Dilbert's world, customers are conspicuously absent. They never appear, and no one ever talks about them. The primary focus is on the jumbled, often pathological, comings and goings of Dilbert and his colleagues. While this works well as a source of humor for the comic strip, it would not last long in the marketplace. Good businesses put the customer ahead of internal tensions and squabbling. They work to prevent irrational forces from undermining why the enterprise exists. But it's easier said than done. In Chapter 8, we discuss ideas and strategies for building structure that works for us more than against us.

ESCAPING CLUELESSNESS VII: UNDERSTANDING HIERARCHY

- POSITION SHAPES BEHAVIOR.
- HIERARCHY CREATES MONARCHS, LORDS, AND SERFS IN MODERN ORGANIZATIONS.
- TO ESCAPE UNPRODUCTIVE FEUDALISM:
  - STUDY THE SYSTEM.
  - STOP BLAMING.
  - SWIM UPSTREAM—OR STEP OUT OF THE FLOW.
- WE ALL WANT CLARITY AND PREDICTABILITY BUT HATE RED TAPE; EFFECTIVE STRUCTURES BALANCE EFFICIENCY AND FLEXIBILITY.
- DESIGN STRUCTURE AROUND THE CUSTOMER TO MAXIMIZE BENEFITS AND MINIMIZE COSTS OF BUREAUCRACY.

8

Shaping Structures That Work

Have you ever wished you could work someplace that had less confusion, more clarity, and a clearer sense of direction? Have you ever been disappointed or embarrassed at the quality of the goods or services your organization provides? Fuzzy focus, internal warfare, and massive waste of time and effort don't add up to a recipe for excellence. Irrational workplaces may thrive and persist in movies, TV, and comic pages, but don't do so well in the intensely competitive world of modern enterprise.

One distinctive feature of top-performing teams or organizations is a goal-directed, reasonably clear, well-coordinated structure that draws the best from people and harmonizes their individual efforts into a productive whole. Goods or services delivered by a confused and chaotic organization sink like a stone as customers and clients flee elsewhere. We're all like Berman in Chapter 7: We get fed up pretty fast with organizations that can't give us what we really want.

Getting the design right is hard because every workplace has to wrestle with basic structural dilemmas. Some places handle them pretty well. Others, like Dilbert's digs, fall considerably short. Dilbert feels in control of his destiny only in his cubicle. In one strip, he stares at his computer, thinking: "I am king of my cubicle, the absolute ruler of this tiny realm . . . and these are my loyal subjects: master computer, mister stapler, and the binder family." Wally appears at the entrance wondering who spilled the coffee. The brown stains are Dilbert's virtual moat, his way of thwarting barbarians at the gate of his cubicle castle. In his diminutive domain, he's insulated from lords, other serfs—even the monarch. But cubicle confinement breeds more isolation and disconnection than teamwork and productivity.

FRANK 'N' HOPE: *RULING THE ROOST*

Hope: Sounds a lot like you, Frank. King of your cubicle. Ruler of your realm, with your computer, stapler, and binders.

Frank: I've spilled enough coffee to make my own moat. To keep you and the other barbarians at bay.

Hope: Ever get lonely in there?

Frank: No chance with you coming by to preach all the time.

Your place may be reasonably orderly. Or it may feel like one of those scenes of urban chaos from films like *Godzilla* or *Independence Day*—monsters or aliens wreaking havoc, buildings crumbling, vehicles crashing, and people panicking everywhere. Either way, it helps to understand some structural basics. In this chapter we talk about some of the things that your company should be doing. We also spell out some things you can do to move things in a positive direction.

Every organization has to parcel out work to individuals or groups. The traditional approach is to create different jobs and units, each with its own specialty—such as engineering, information technology, marketing, sales, and management. The premise is that you need a product or service, a specific market to aim at, a sales force to close deals with customers, and a cadre of managers who make decisions and coordinate how the different groups work together. In an ideal world, different units have common goals and work cooperatively. In the real world, they're often at war. Marketing folks see engineers as narrow-minded nerds who wouldn't recognize a customer need if one hit them in the face. The engineers, in turn, view marketers as overpaid glad-handers and air-heads. Sales complains that manufacturing is rigid and slow. Manufacturing thinks salespeople promise the impossible to nail down commissions. The workplace becomes a confused, aimless welter of competing subgroups. Each pursues its own agenda, protects its own turf, and blames somebody else when anything goes wrong. It can be entertaining in movies and comic strips. But if you're trapped there every day, or you're at the receiving end of the company's services or products, it's not so funny.

What do companies do to achieve greater harmony between specialized groups? The oldest and simplest strategy is formal hierarchy and top-down coordination via planning, policies, supervision, and executive decisions. Traditionally, that's been the dominant approach. But it can degenerate into the kind of mindless rigidity we saw in Berman's soap drama. The other way organizations pull things together is through lateral forms of coordination: meetings, teams, matrix arrangements, and the like. In the demanding and turbulent global marketplace, businesses have been relying more and more on lateral coordination. Whatever the mix, the objective is to shape a structure that gives people a chance to do good work. Take Saturn, where an employee once observed, "Given the opportunity, everyone would like to produce a perfect product. At Saturn, they've given us that opportunity—a chance to succeed."

How do organizations help people succeed? Increasingly, high-performing organizations rely on structural approaches that combine clear direction with flexibility and empowerment. In their book *The Wisdom of Teams* (Boston: Harvard Business School Press, 1993), Jon R. Katzenbach and Douglas K. Smith identify the common elements of their strategy:

1. Higher management sets broad goals and general challenges, and then gives lower levels flexibility to work out specifics.
2. Teams and units translate the broader mission into specific, measurable performance goals.
3. Teams assemble the right mix of expertise, crossing functional boundaries as needed to find needed talent.
4. Teams agree on how to work together and develop clear expectations, roles, and relationships.
5. Teams hold themselves collectively accountable for results.

None of this is rocket science. But someone has to understand the basic concept. Few of us have the authority to create dramatic change in our organization's structure. There are plenty of pointy-haired bosses ready to squelch noble efforts from those in the "lowerarchy." But anyone, at any level, can have an impact beyond her individual cubicle. We just have to be realistic about what we're able to influence. Structure is more than red tape and oppressive rules. Don't overlook the possibilities of building structures of roles and relationships that work for people instead of against them.

FRANK 'N' HOPE: *ALL TOGETHER NOW?*

Hope: If you could have the ideal job, what's your wish list?

Frank: Big salary, limo, company jet. And very early retirement.

Hope: Short of that, Frank. What would make your job better?

Frank: Get the boss out of our hair. Let us figure things out for ourselves.

Hope: What about producing something the customer wants? Or making money? That's what management cares about.

Frank: So let them figure it out.

Hope: What if they set the target? Then give us a chance to make it happen. Let us decide how to work together.

Frank: Probably better than drowning in all the pigeon droppings they dump on us now.

Hope: We could all fly or fall together.

Frank: Don't hold your breath. The concept is way too sensible for the bosses.

We're all ambivalent about bureaucracy. On the one hand, we rail against its restrictions and red tape. It's a convenient scapegoat that usually produces universal head nodding. On the other hand, we also know the frustration of trying to get work done when goals are fuzzy or conflicting, responsibilities are poorly defined, other people's work clashes with ours, and no one knows who's in charge. Such conditions are a recipe for confusion and conflict in both families and workplaces. The challenge is to find the right balance between repression and anarchy, capriciousness and creativity, top-down rigidity and bottom-up chaos.

On the sports field, no team wants to lose because players didn't know the rules of the game, were in positions that didn't fit their talents, or weren't willing to be team players. Fans get incensed when they see ragtag, uncoordinated play. But, somehow, we lose sight of all this when we get to work. We're more willing to put up with dysfunction or a lack of teamwork. Too often we're passively resigned to living with chaos or waiting for our boss to do something. Everyone suffers in the resulting stand-off. What are the alternatives? What can be done to create a more focused, better integrated, higher performing workplace? Common sense from experience outside work provides some possibilities. Both employees and managers can take initiatives. Asking forgiveness rather than permission is sometimes very wise.

1. *Set or clarify goals.* Think of a United Way campaign with no financial target. Imagine, if you can, Michael Jordan (before he retired) approaching a new basketball season with a goal of, "Win some and lose some, maybe make the playoffs if we're lucky." Deep down, people are goal-directed. They'll rally to the cause if they know what it is and care about it. Organizational goals are too often confining, con-

fusing, or conflicting. A college president once said ruefully that the real goals of the university seemed to be providing parking for faculty, football for alumni, and sex for students. A little jaundiced? Maybe, but there's a grain of truth there. Just don't move too far down the cynical path. The trick is to set specific, measurable goals that focus people's energy. When Gordon Bethune became CEO at Continental Airlines, he took responsibility for an enterprise that made even Dilbert's cubicle world look good. By most measures, Continental was the worst airline in North America. Bethune helped turn a dismal operation around by setting some clear goals: be on time, provide clean planes and good food, treat passengers right, and get their bags to the right destination. Simple stuff that paved the way to profitability and to surprising the industry by being named America's best airline in 1997. From worst to first.

But goals don't always have to flow from corporate headquarters. Even low-level serfs in backwater operations can set some goals for themselves. In a famous doll factory experiment, responsibility for setting performance goals was given to women on an assembly line. They were authorized to set the speed of the line and paid according to how well they achieved their targets. Production soared, as did their paychecks. What might happen if some of the people you work with conspired to do something productive instead of looking for ways to outwit their boss? The boss might either take credit or faint, but it might pay off.

2. *Shape a structure that fits.* How do you decide what structure you need? A workable structure responds to the task at hand, the people who will do it, and the demands of the environment. Clear-cut, top-down, standardized approaches often work well for routine tasks and stable environments (such as manufacturing paper clips or adjusting

insurance claims). Unpredictable, fast-changing, hard-to-read situations (such as an Internet start-up company) require work arrangements that are flatter, more fluid, and controlled by lateral give-and-take and professional norms. The contrasting structures of two familiar forms of work—hamburgers and health care—illustrate the point.

McDonald's, the company that made the Big Mac a household word, dominates the fast-food business around the globe. McDonald's grew into a fast-food giant with a tightly controlled, top-down structure. A relatively small staff at its world headquarters outside Chicago made most of the key decisions for all of the employees spread across thousands of local outlets in the United States and, eventually, the world. In its early years, McDonald's built its success on a simple, cookie-cutter model: Every restaurant imitated the look, prices, and product line of the wildly successful, original McDonald's restaurant in San Bernadino, California.

McDonald's managers and employees have limited discretion about how to do their jobs. Much of their work is controlled by technology; machines time french fries and measure soft drinks. Cooks are not expected to develop creative new versions of Big Macs or Quarter-Pounders (although the Egg McMuffin and other innovations were created by local franchises). The parent company has elaborate systems to ensure that food and service conform to standard specifications. Buy a Big Mac in New York or Los Angeles, Hong Kong or Moscow, and it'll taste pretty similar. Historically, McDonald's made little effort to offer special products in different markets. The McDonald's on the Champs Elysées in Paris makes few concessions to French culinary style.

For physicians, the work situation is vastly different. Doctors have great discretion in how they do their work.

Individual patients present an enormous variety of health histories and needs. Sometimes they arrive with clearly defined symptoms of well-understood conditions, and the doctor can quickly develop a diagnosis and treatment plan. But doctors really earn their money when symptoms are vague or contradictory, so that it's difficult to pin down what's really going on and what to do about it. The essence of doctors' work is using their professional judgment and skill in tailoring their response to the specific needs of individual patients. Physicians' offices are set up to let doctors concentrate on what they do best, while off-loading more routine tasks such as scheduling and patient-billing to support staff.

Fast food chains and physicians' offices both get their jobs done because they have shaped distinctive structures that work for:

- What they do—the predictability of burgers and fries vs. the infinite variety of patients and health needs
- Their goals—making a buck vs. improving health
- Their workforce—low-skill, entry-level servers vs. physician professionals

The basic lesson is pretty clear: Effective structures are determined by what you're trying to do, the goals you have in mind, and the people you're working with. The traditional, top-down pyramid works for concrete tasks, specific goals, and less-skilled workers. For ambiguous projects, multiple or ambiguous objectives, and a highly professional workforce, you need a flatter, laterally governed, fluid work environment.

To underline the point, consider what happened to McDonald's as it evolved into a global company with restaurants in virtually every major city in the world. Selling burgers and fries in the United States was a relatively straightforward and predictable business from one coast to the other. But what you do in a country like India, where cows are sacred and much of the population is vegetarian? (McDonald's answer was Mutton Macs and Veggie Burgers.) How do you respond to differences in tastes across cultures and continents? Globalization made the McDonald's environment more complex and turbulent. To fit the new circumstances, McDonald's had to loosen up the model that had made it so successful. James Cantalupo, head of McDonald's International, underscored the transition in a 1996 interview with T. L. Friedman in *The New York Times:* "McDonald's stands for a lot more than just hamburgers and American fast food. Cultural sensitivity is part of it too. There is no 'Euroburger.' We have a different chicken sandwich in England than we do in Germany. We are trying not to think as a cookie cutter."*

For doctors, it's been going the other way. In recent years, the drive for efficiencies and cost savings has led managed care organizations to try to control and standardize doctor's performance. They ask their physicians to prescribe only drugs on an approved list and to offer only services that the health maintenance organization (HMO) recognizes as appropriate and cost-effective. The health-care organizations' push for tighter structure has collided head-on with physicians' desire to protect their professional discretion and autonomy. That battle is likely to continue for the foreseeable future, with patients caught somewhere in the middle. As hamburgers and health care illustrate, getting the right structure is vital. But even if you succeed, it won't stay right indefinitely. Sooner or later, the world will change on you.

*"Big Mac II," *The New York Times,* December 11, 1996, p. A21.

When change does hit, it's rarely easy to deal with it. Flatter and more fluid sound fine until the change hits you where you live. Consider a recent conversation between a manager and an operator in a printing plant. For years, workers had moved in a predictable progression through a series of different assignments. But technological changes were making the old machines obsolete. The manager asked the operator about his career goals.

"I want to move over there to Press 6 when that job opens up," said the worker.

"But," asked the manager, "what would you want to do if that press isn't there any more?"

The answer was immediate, "I still want to work on Press 6."

The world is changing—whether we're ready or not.

The basic structural principles that apply to hamburgers and health care are just as important in organizing a team or a workgroup. No recipe works universally. Every group needs to assess its task and circumstances and develop a blend of vertical and lateral approaches that make sense. If the structure in your team or unit is breaking down, don't just wait for a new blueprint to arrive from on high. See what you can do locally to get things back into shape. Start with some basic questions: What's the nature of our work? Is our environment static or fluid? How are we structured now? What different arrangements might we consider for better performance?

3. *Put people in the right positions.* Hiring good people is an important first step. But once lured, they have to be placed in a job that takes advantage of their talents. In Chapter 5, we watched as Susan discussed a possible promotion with Dale. Susan was pretty sure she was moving Dale into a job he wasn't ready for, but she did it anyway. The match be-

tween job and person is crucial to performance. Getting into the wrong job harms both you and the organization. If you're a manager, you bear a responsibility for shaping a job to the person who's in it. As an employee you need to think about what's right for you. A position that helps you both succeed and learn is the best of all possible worlds. Take the initiative and make a realistic case for why your position should be revamped, or why you're right for a different job. Don't simply wait passively for management to discover your talents or move you into the job of your dreams.

4. *Clarify your work relationship with others.* On any team, people need to know how their work relates to the work of others (see Figure 8-1). Without coordination and teamwork, the best individual efforts produce a poor outcome. Take the Chicago Bulls team that dominated the National Basketball Association (NBA) for much of the 1990s. The conventional wisdom was that anyone could win with Michael Jordan. But Jordan and his teammates saw it differently. As one of them put it, "Most teams have guys who want to win, but aren't willing to do what it takes. What it takes is to give yourself over to the team and play your part. That may

Figure 8-1. It helps to know who's doing what.

not always make you happy, but you've got to do it. Because when you do, that's when you win."* The same message emerged from the championship game of the 1998 soccer World Cup. Brazil had the superstars, but France won with a better team effort. Maybe you remember a time your inspired efforts flopped because someone else got in your way or didn't come through as they were supposed to. When an American Airlines plane docks at a Dallas gate, for example, more than twenty coordinated functions—food service, refueling, baggage handling, many more—are needed to ensure a seamless flight. If you fly enough, you've seen just about all of them go wrong—the plane is delayed while they wait for a missing crew member, someone else is in your assigned spot, your seat is broken, the food runs out before they get to you, the flight attendant is mad at the world and spills tomato soup on your jacket, the restrooms are a mess, the jetway is broken, your baggage is mistakenly diverted to Finland, and so on. It only takes one foul-up to spoil the whole experience.

We often think that coordination is solely management's job. They're supposed to write the policies, issue the commands, and create the systems to make sure everyone's on the same page. Sometimes bosses live up to those expectations. Often they don't. If you're in a group where people are constantly stepping on others' toes or pointing fingers of blame, try an experiment. See if you can identify structural glitches that could be fixed. Take a risk. Even if it doesn't work, things will be no worse than before. If it clicks, you're a star—maybe even on a management fast track.

But how, you ask? Choose an issue or task where there is continual confusion or conflict. Create a matrix listing re-

*Quoted in P. Jackson, *Sacred Hoops: Spiritual Lessons of a Hardwood Warrior* (New York: Hyperion, 1995).

sponsibilities in the far-left column. In the remaining columns, place individual roles across the top. Now have everyone individually assign a letter to each person for every responsibility. Give "R" to the person who's responsible or accountable for how the activity goes—the one with the monkey on his or her back. Now assign letters to specify that person's relationships to others. Give an "I" to anyone who is to be kept informed, a "C "to anyone who needs to be consulted, an "A" to anyone who has to approve what's done, and an "O" to an individual (or group) who is essentially "out of the loop." It's called the CAIRO process (putting the letters together in a memorable acronym), and it's very revealing. It goes beyond the organization chart to pinpoint what people are expected to do and how they relate to others. Any employee can initiate the activity. Management blessing isn't essential, though it helps to have them involved.

CAIRO usually produces several important discoveries. It shows that people have very different views of how things are supposed to work. It reveals who's overloaded and underused, how many levels of approval someone needs to get before taking action, and who appears to need control over the operations. The exercise can clarify why people are at each other's throats, why things are rarely getting done, and why high quality products and services are not being produced. The same basic issues of who's supposed to do what are as important at home as they are at work. Since almost all of us have lived in families of one kind or another, let's look at how a fairly typical family approaches decisions about where to go on vacation. Table 8-1 lists the four players in this particular soap opera, and shows how each of them thinks decisions are supposed to happen.

As Mom sees it, Dad's responsible for developing plans, but she has to approve, and the kids have to be consulted

Table 8-1. It helps to know who's doing what.

	Cairo Roles			
As Seen By:	*Mom*	*Dad*	*Sis*	*Bro*
Mom	Approve	Responsible	Consulted	Consulted
Dad	Consulted	Responsible	Informed	Informed
Sis	Responsible	Consulted	Consulted	Consulted
Bro	Informed	Responsible	Informed	Approve

before anything is finalized. Dad agrees that he's responsible, but he thinks he only needs to consult Mom and inform the kids. Sis, on the other hand, believes Mom's responsible for making the decision after consulting everyone else. And Bro, egocentric male adolescent that he is, assumes that he has the right to approve or disapprove whatever plan Dad makes. Whereupon they can tell the womenfolk. In a typical year, the scenario plays out roughly like this: Dad develops a plan and consults Mom, who tells him she'd rather do something else. Dad figures he's fulfilled his responsibility to consult, makes minor modifications, and proceeds to book the trip and put down deposits. Mom stews because Dad went ahead with a plan that she hadn't approved. Sis hates the plan and is angry that she wasn't consulted. She mostly blames Mom because, in Sis's mind, Mom's responsible for these decisions. Bro is furious that the family made a vacation decision without his approval. Once the vacation gets under way, Dad is enthusiastic, and everyone else is chronically grumpy. Bro sulks. Mom and Sis argue. Eventually, Dad's cheerfulness evaporates and he launches a tirade about living with a family of whiners and ingrates. As often happens in both families and workplaces, people blame each other. No one recognizes the underlying structural problem: The family has never sat down to get clear on how vacation decisions will be made.

FRANK 'N' HOPE: *TIME FOR CAIRO?*

Hope:	How was your vacation, Frank?
Frank:	Too short. And too expensive.
Hope:	Where'd you go?
Frank:	Where my wife wanted. Like always.
Hope:	She chooses the place and you pay?
Frank:	She's stubborn!
Hope:	Time for CAIRO?
Frank:	Don't even mention the word. Next thing you know, she'll be planning a trip to Egypt.

Getting the roles right makes a big difference. A while back, Trans World Airlines (TWA) found that passenger complaints were soaring. One problem was all the approval levels that passenger-service personnel had to go through before doing anything. Lost your bags? Let me call my supervisor. Been bumped? Hang on while I see what I can do. Irate? Stew awhile while I try to get approval for something to make things better. By giving more discretion to the front line, TWA improved customer satisfaction. Lost your bags? Here's a voucher to buy necessities. Got bumped? Here's a meal voucher, and if we can't get you out tonight, we'll put you up in a hotel at our expense. Pissed off? We screwed up, I'm sorry, and here's a coupon for a free flight.

Continental CEO Gordon Bethune provided an even more vivid example. He and a group of employees gathered all the policy manuals and burned them in the company parking lot. Message: When dealing with a passenger, we want you to think. It's your responsibility to do what's appropriate on the spot.

In many workplaces, people are off the hook. They don't have to take responsibility. They leave it all to the boss and then chuckle when he does something stupid. Some hard, authentic discussions about other possibilities can be highly productive. Management doesn't have to do everything. Someone's got to take the bull by the horns. You may be as likely a candidate as anyone else. At home, at play, and at work, too many chronic problems are caused by poorly designed structures that made everyone either a villain or victim.

5. *Reward people for (the right) performance.* If you give people responsibility, you need to offer something in return. Sometimes there's the sheer joy of doing a good job. There's also the pat on the back and other forms of thanks for a job well done. Both are important, but they're no substitute for decent wages and benefits. It's a key management responsibility and a basic employee right. How to reward good performance is a tougher call. Some gurus advocate individual bonuses. Others argue for group awards. Which you choose depends on what you value. Need individual achievement? Reward individuals. Team performance what it takes? The group gets the bucks. Individual incentives work best when it's more important for individuals to maximize their own performance than to work well with one another, as with sales people who work separate territories, or baseball players. But beware of the risk that individual incentives can spawn unproductive conflict or lead employees to cut corners and lose sight of the big picture in a single-minded pursuit of more money.

Think of a basketball or soccer team where everyone wants to score, but no one wants to pass. Team performance goes downhill fast. Phil Jackson, in his previously quoted book *Sacred Hoops,* lamented the perverse incentives in the NBA: "Superstars with dramatic, eye-catching moves are paid vast sums of money, while players who contribute to the team effort in less flamboyant ways often make close to the minimum salary. As a result, few players come to the NBA dreaming of becoming good team players. It's difficult, sometimes impossible, to get players to check their inflated egos at the gym door." It's no surprise that one study found that "most individual merit or performance-based pay plans share two attributes: they absorb vast amounts of management time and resources, and they make everybody unhappy."*

Saturn, GM's novel experiment in organizing people, rewards the group. A sizable chunk of compensation is at risk each year, for both employees and managers. If the corporation succeeds, everyone benefits. In years past, each employee received a substantial bonus. When performance falls below expectations, everyone takes the hit. In 1997, for example, Saturn employees earned less than other GM workers. But in previous years they'd earned more.

A second challenge in rewarding performance is making sure that what you reward is really what you want. A lot of organizations get this wrong. The most common mistake is rewarding things that are easy to count and measure, regardless of whether they're what's really important. The old Soviet system, for example, often rewarded factories for quantity but ignored quality. The predictable result was vast quantities of junk: defective concrete, cars that fell apart, and toilet paper you had to be pretty desperate to use. Same thing

*Jeffrey Pfeffer, "Six Dangerous Myths About Pay," *Harvard Business Review,* May-June 1998, pp. 108–119.

with Internal Revenue Service (IRS) auditors who were judged on the basis of how much money they extracted from each taxpayer, but not on how they did it. Agents in some offices resorted to a variety of abusive or illegal practices in an effort to get the numbers up. The resulting excesses led to heavy damage for the agency in Congressional hearings.

A third key with rewards is making sure that they're really rewards. If the company gives you some time off when you really wanted a pat on the back, or gives you a pay raise that's so small it feels more like an insult than an incentive, it won't do much for motivation. It's important to pay enough attention to the people you work with to know what's important to them and what isn't. If you assume that one reward fits everyone, you're bound to make at least some people unhappy. As a potential recipient, it's equally important to let others know what's important to you and what isn't.

Structure can work for us and against us, although we're much more likely to notice it when it misfires or gets in our way. There are good rules and bad ones. Brilliant meetings and disasters. Sometimes people in authority know what they are doing; other times they haven't a clue. More discretion for employees sometimes pays off big. Other times it leads to mammoth screw-ups. Modern workplaces have both good goals and bad. The good ones are put on public display as virtues. Shadier ambitions are hidden backstage. A workable balance between "boy scout" public virtues and the "real objectives" provides a reasonable focus that people can honor and accept. At work, as at home, finding the right balance is an ongoing struggle. It doesn't do any good to label all structure as bureaucracy and red tape. You need to make structure work for you. That's not the sole province of management or employees. It's an ongoing dance. When the dance goes well, it shapes arrangements that generally work. Not all the time, and not for everyone. But for most people most of the time. It only happens when cubicle and corporation stop blaming and learn to dance together.

ESCAPING CLUELESSNESS VIII: SHAPING STRUCTURE TO CIRCUMSTANCES

- BAD STRUCTURES HARM BOTH PEOPLE AND PRODUCTIVITY.
- STRUCTURE DEPENDS ON CIRCUMSTANCES:
  - TOP-DOWN, VERTICAL CONTROL WORKS BEST FOR SIMPLE TASKS IN STABLE ENVIRONMENTS.
  - TURBULENT, FAST-CHANGING SITUATIONS CALL FOR FLATTER, MORE FLUID STRUCTURES.
- IMPROVE STRUCTURE BY:
  - SETTING CLEAR GOALS
  - ALIGNING STRUCTURE TO SITUATION
  - PUTTING PEOPLE IN THE RIGHT JOB
  - REWARDING PERFORMANCE
  - CLARIFYING RELATIONSHIPS

Looking Ahead

- Traditional, top-down bureaucracy is a dying breed.
- Organizations of the future will be flatter, more flexible, and more complicated.
- The good news for employees: more autonomy and influence.
- The bad news: less job security, more change and unpredictability.

SUGGESTIONS FOR FURTHER READING

A classic piece highlighting the importance of fitting structure to the business environment is the book by Paul Lawrence and Jay Lorsch, *Organization and Environment.* Henry Mintzberg's *Structure in Fives: Designing Effective Organizations* offers an elaborated update.

See the Bibliography for publication details of these books.

PART V

CRACKING THE CULTURAL CODE

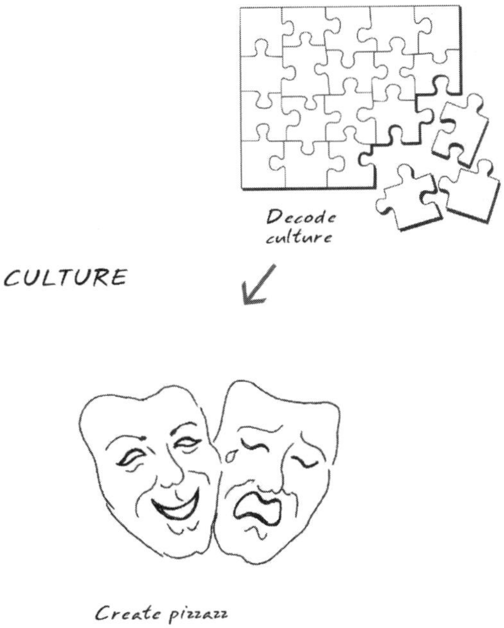

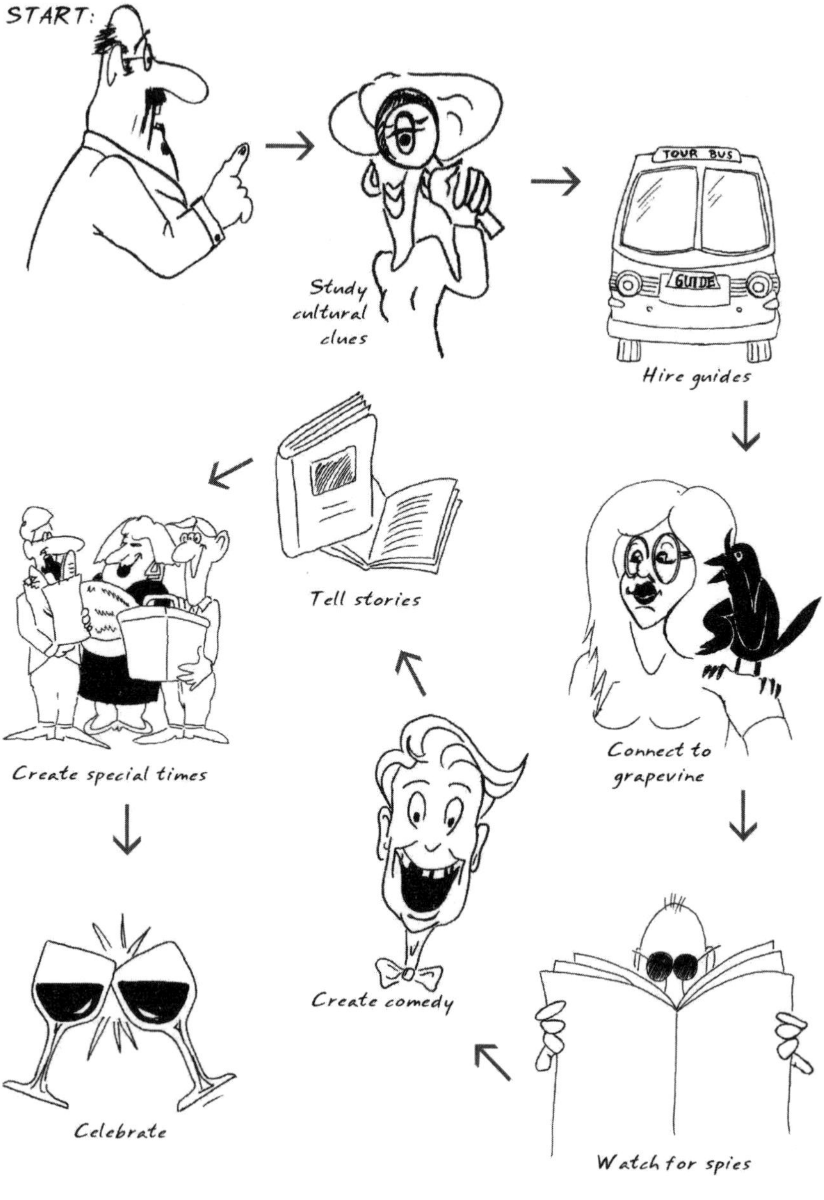
START:
TOUR BUS
GUIDE
Study cultural clues
Hire guides
Connect to grapevine
Watch for spies
Create comedy
Tell stories
Create special times
Celebrate

9

Cracking the Hidden Code: Becoming a Cultural Sleuth

Ever had a day at the office where nothing seemed to make any sense? Have you and your colleagues ever puzzled about why certain things never change even though they don't work as they're supposed to? Have you ever felt that your coworkers seem to obey some unwritten, secret code, even though no one knows quite why?

Workplaces are often weird. Projects are assigned and then forgotten. Status reports are required but never read. Information is collected and then ignored. Meetings go on for hours but nothing gets done. People talk at length without saying anything. Employees wander around in a continual state of puzzlement and discontent. If you look deeper, though, there's sense in the senselessness. Just as fish don't notice water, we don't always see taken-for-granted patterns that govern everyday action. Nor do we see alternatives—things we could do to improve our lot at work.

Things get much clearer when you learn to decipher the subtle or hidden cultural clues that abound in any office—artifacts, behavior, language, dress, and ritualized intermissions such as coffee breaks, lunch, and the late afternoon watering hole. Cracking the cultural code reveals the real stuff that lurks just under the surface of everyday life. You understand more, and you can cope better—or know that it's time to leave. As we've noted before, you always have the options to sign up, speak up, sign off, or ship out. It's easier to choose if you know what you're up against.

We're all social animals. We crave belongingness and meaning. We depend on the people around us to help us find both. Collectively, we create culture, accepted ways of doing things (see Figure 9-1). We do it through trial and error. In the course of everyday experience, every group and organization gleans lessons about what works and what flops. Over

Figure 9-1. The power of culture.

"I don't know how it started, either. All I know is that it's part of our corporate culture."

time, we accumulate a history that gradually shapes who we are, what we value, how we think, and how we do things. To reinforce our evolving values and beliefs, we identify human icons—heroes and heroines who embody the best, devils who exemplify the worst. Culture is hard to experience or share in words, so we create rituals and ceremonies—occasions where we bond to one another and share our commitment to something bigger. We also share stories. They're fun, and, more important, they carry valuable lessons. Culture provides the symbolic glue that holds people and organizations together. In many places, the glue doesn't stick very well. It's more like what you find on the back of a Post-it. But it still helps people learn the ropes, even in a day-to-day life that may look very strange to outsiders.

How do you crack the cultural code at work? Try being a cultural anthropologist for a day. Unless you're an air traffic controller or a brain surgeon, no one is likely to notice that you're taking time to study the natives' folkways rather than focusing strictly on the task at hand.

1. *Study cultural clues.* Open your senses fully and try to take nothing for granted. Notice the architecture—space speaks. Before Hurricane Andrew, Burger King's headquarters in Florida was a feudal kingdom. Expansive executive offices on one floor facing the ocean, everyone else in cramped quarters. After the hurricane devastated the headquarters building, it was rebuilt. In the new building, secretaries and functional people have offices with an ocean view. Executives who travel most of the time occupy small interior offices. The new spatial arrangements reflect a sea change in cultural values. Before, status ruled. Your position in the pecking order determined your perks. Now, space is aligned

with what people do. Contribution to overall effectiveness is what counts.

What do you notice about the building in which you work? When you get off the elevator or come off the stairs, what leaps out? How does the place look? How does it smell? What sounds, if any, strike you? Walk around to get the lay of the landscape. Who has the big corner offices? Who gets a tiny cubicle? Notice artifacts. What's on the walls? What do people keep on their desks? Any graffiti in the rest rooms? Check out wastebaskets. What do people toss as opposed to keep?

Hang around as people go through their daily doings. Observe meetings. Who arrives late? Who sits where? Who leaves early? How long do meetings last? Do they start on time? Who talks? Who doesn't? Who's listened to or ignored? In one big computer company, meetings always start fifteen minutes late. In the new Continental Airlines, meetings always start on time, to signal the importance of on-time performance. What are the preferred media—flip charts, color slides, computer graphics, or blackboards? In one merger of two companies, a problem became apparent right away. One company relied on multicolored 35mm slides. The other favored simple flip charts. Until they worked it out, meetings were a war zone. Hang out around the water cooler or coffee pot, if one exists. Who shows up at which times? What informal subgroups are apparent? Are subgroups formed around race, gender, position, or function? Do smokers have their own gathering place? As a noted anthropologist tried to pinpoint a company's subcultures, she had trouble figuring out why one subgroup was so cohesive. It turned out they all smoked. Since their office is smoke-free, they gather outside before work, at lunch, and during breaks. This gives them countless opportunities to gab, gossip, and plot.

How do people communicate? Face-to-face? E-mail? Memo? What do they say? Listen for pronouns, slang, acronyms, profanity. "I want this done" is very different from "How should we do this?" "This is the way we do things around here" conveys a different attitude than "Shine on and keep your head down." What metaphors are evident in discourse? Sports (slam dunks and goal-line stands)? Military (frontal assaults and sneak attacks)?

What do people wear? Do engineers wear regulation costumes—short-sleeve shirts, plastic pocket protectors, and skimpy, nondescript ties? Or are they more often in T-shirts and cutoffs? Do bosses wear standard-issue dark suits? Or aloha shirts? Do women managers dress much like their male counterparts? Or do they favor colors and styles you'd rarely find in a men's department? In the IBM of old, white shirts and dark suits were standard. One recruit showed up in tweed for his first day on the job. His boss asked him where he found the slacks to go with his sport coat. The new hire picked up the signal immediately. In a similar experience, one of us showed up for an evening dinner at a well-known advertising firm wearing a light tan suit. Everyone else was in blue pinstripes. A vice-president highlighted our violation of the dress code by asking, "Where do you get your suits bleached?"

What rituals draw people together? Are they held before or after work? At noon over lunch? Does the work itself serve as a ritual as people bond around success or failure? The sign of a ritual is that the same things occur over and over, but with a deeper, more special feeling than mere routine. Rituals typically occur at the day's beginning, end, or midpoint. Notice who attends and who's excluded, and how. What symbols dominate the ritualistic exchange? Coffee and cookies? Wine and cheese? Fancy slides and sophisticated analyses? Each Friday night at Southwest Airline's Love Field Headquarters, employees gather around a barbecue grill. They cook, quaff, chew, and chat, informally mulling over the week's events. Before an operation, surgeons often scrub for a traditional seven minutes, even though modern soaps kill germs in about thirty seconds. The scrub helps the operating team prepare for the delicate task ahead.

What does the culture celebrate? Individual achievement? Collective triumph? Seasonal occasions like holiday parties or summer outings? Corporate anniversaries or individual birthdays? Southwest Airlines celebrates them all, which is one of the reasons that the airline's spirit is so robust and contagious. Do people gather when things get tough? What happens when the inevitable screw-up occurs? One large U.S. retail firm gathers periodically to celebrate its mistakes. The message: We're human and blow it once in a while. But we learn from our errors. When tough decisions are announced, what do people do? Are the downsized honored with a dignified send-off? Are mergers marked with appropriate transition rites? Two large hospitals celebrated their merger with a hilarious video showing the two CEOs being surgically joined at the hip. Do celebrations have sustaining oomph? Or do people just go through the motions?

Your own observations will yield thousands of clues to help penetrate fog-shrouded cultural practices. But there's more you can do. Every workplace has a cast of characters who can become your informal guides.

2. *Hire guides: priests and storytellers.* There's a cast of characters in every workplace who can be recruited as cultural guides. Locate informal priests or priestesses. Don't look in a big corner office. Priests are more likely to be typing away in a small cubicle, or closeted somewhere in the archives. They're often old-timers who came in with the furni-

ture. The reigning priestess of a California medical center was the head of housekeeping. She could easily cross subcultural boundaries and served as a passionate promoter of the hospital's core mission. One of Anheuser-Busch's priests was an 84-year-old retired brewmaster. He came to work each day and held court. Priests regularly take confessions and are widely respected throughout the organization. They are keepers of history and protectors of tradition. They can tell you how things came to be and instruct you in prevailing cultural mores and norms. Be reverent, pay attention, and you'll find a storehouse of knowledge and wisdom, both ancient and modern. You can also make a friend whose counsel and support could be a big help somewhere down the line.

Look too for corporate storytellers; individuals who dramatize everyday exploits and perpetuate corporate lore. Their legendary tales carry grains of truth about important values and taboos. Take storytellers to the local watering hole. Listen to their tales and read between the lines. You'll get important lessons on how to get ahead and what to avoid. You'll hear things you'd almost never find in policy manuals or official publications. Stories make lessons real and memorable. Even though unofficial, the lessons are often right on. The stories will tell you about heroes and heroines—the living logos who exemplify what the organization stands for. Dilbert, for example, is a cultural hero because he exemplifies the pains and frustrations of cubicle life and regularly outwits the boss in the process. In other settings, heroes and heroines represent significant values like hard work, creativity, or courage. There was an employee at 3M many years ago who stubbornly championed the newfangled idea of clear adhesive tape. His boss didn't see any value in it and told him to work on something else. The employee quietly went on working on his tape. He was fired for insubordination, but came back to work the next day anyway. His embarrassed supervisors put him back on the payroll and asked him just to leave others alone. His idea flowered into Scotch tape—one of 3M's greatest and most enduring product triumphs. That stubborn employee became a cultural icon, an exemplar of the values of creativity and persistence. Years later, his example inspired another stubborn 3Mer to persist in looking for some way to use an adhesive he'd discovered that didn't stick very well. Along came another 3Mer who sang in a church choir. He was looking for bookmarks that wouldn't fall out of hymnals. Of that union was born the Post-it note.

On the other hand, you might find that the heroes in your workplace are folks who toe the line and kiss up to the boss. If that's what gets rewarded, but it's not your style, you've learned an important lesson. Maybe you need to find somewhere else to work.

3. *Connect with grapevine gossips.* Gossips are always privy to the latest scoop, even things that are supposed to be confidential or hush-hush. Hear them out and you'll often get the best briefing going. Their accuracy isn't perfect, but they're reliable clues about salient issues, concerns, hopes, and fears in your workplace. If you hear a story about how the CEO chewed out a VP in a hotel corridor, the details may be distorted, but you can be pretty sure something big is afoot. Rumors of impending layoffs may be exaggerated, but you'd be wise to prepare for rough seas. Gossip is a two-way street. You have to give in order to receive. Don't be too cautious about divulging a few things yourself. Chances are the truth will be less harmful than what the gossips make up on their own. A few minutes over coffee with your local gossip is often worth more than a multitude of meetings and memos. Information is power. Being up-to-date and in the loop gives you a real advantage over people who rely solely

on the official channels to keep on top of things. And if there are things you'd like people to be talking about, there's no better place than the grapevine to get the word out. Plant your story with people who are sure to spread the word.

4. *Watch for spies.* Finally, be alert to signs of the clandestine intelligence network—the world of spies and counterspies. Most executives have spies, and employees often have a "mole" planted in the boss's corner office. Some organizations even create internal counterespionage units. The secret world of intelligence gathering and espionage isn't necessarily good or bad. It just is. It can work for you or against you. You want to be careful about what you say to anyone who might be a spy. But if you know who the agents are, you can judiciously plant some seeds that might grow nicely for you.

FRANK 'N' HOPE: *GIRL SCOUT?*

Hope: I've been doing some scouting.

Frank: So now you're a girl scout! You could start a troop and give out merit badges.

Hope: I might if I thought you'd buy some cookies. But cut the sarcasm and you might learn something.

Frank: Like what?

Hope: You know Liz in security?

Frank: Not very well. Should I?

Hope: You're missing an opportunity. She sure knows you. There isn't too much she doesn't know.

Frank: She's been here about ninety years.

Hope: She talks to people. And they talk to her. When I want the real scoop, I talk to Liz.

Frank: You'd do about as well talking to my dog.

Hope: He snarls too much. And Liz has better stories. If you wanna know who's moving ahead, who's topped out and why, Liz is amazing.

Frank: She say anything about me?

5. *Form cabals*. Finally, don't be reluctant to form cabals —groups of like-minded people who join together to launch cultural conspiracies. They share common values and have shared interests in pushing the culture in a certain way. Cabal members may seem to have little in common, yet they share a passion for something intrinsic. Southwest Airlines has an

officially sanctioned cabal known as the Culture Committee. It includes representatives from across the company's levels and functions. The only membership requirement is a big heart. Virginia Mason Hospital and Clinic sponsored a similar committee in the 1980s. Its membership included nurses, doctors, technicians, administrators, and staff. The group had a good time planning good times for the hospital. Joining a cabal can supplement your efforts with the collective energy to influence workplace agenda and events.

Together, the characters in the informal cultural network can offer you a comprehensive picture of what works below the surface or behind the scenes. Knowing these taken-for-granted traditional ways and unofficial cultural rules provides a welcome escape from cluelessness. The clues are often subtle, but they're always there. They just need to be gathered and arranged in a cohesive pattern. Reading a culture gives you a chance to be better prepared, less stressed, and less often surprised. Equally important, knowing the existential underbelly offers opportunities to shape as well as be shaped by cultural patterns and rules.

ESCAPING CLUELESSNESS IX: UNCOVERING HIDDEN TRIBAL WAYS

- EVERY GROUP AND ORGANIZATION CREATES CULTURAL WAYS TO MAKE SENSE AND GIVE MEANING TO LIFE AND WORK.
- CULTURAL WAYS AND TRADITIONS DICTATE WHAT PEOPLE WEAR, HOW THEY SPEAK AND WHAT THEY DO.
- UNDERSTANDING CULTURE REDUCES SURPRISE AND STRESS, INCREASES UNDERSTANDING AND CONFIDENCE.
- STUDY CULTURAL CLUES:
  - ENLIST GUIDES.
  - CONNECT TO THE GRAPEVINE.
  - WATCH FOR SPIES.
  - FORM CABALS.
- KNOWING THE EXISTENTIAL UNDERBELLY LETS YOU SHAPE AS WELL AS BE SHAPED BY CULTURE.

10

Creating Pizzazz in a Sterile or Toxic Workplace

How much of your life will be spent at work? Half? Two-thirds? It's a big chunk. If you spend it feeling bored and unappreciated, or you just put in time for a paycheck, you're pouring most of your years down the drain. Weekends and a couple of weeks of vacation a year are pretty meager compensation for forty years with your nose to an unfulfilling grindstone.

What's the alternative? One possibility is to go to work for one of the companies that are finding ways to infuse the workplace with more passion and purpose. A second option is to take the initiative yourself, and experiment with creative ways to build more zest and spirit in your current job. But how do you find or build a meaningful workplace? There are no easy answers, but consider the possibilities below.

If you're ready to look for a better place to work, there are some bright spots out there. They've stumbled onto a blinding revelation—that if you treat employees like dirt, there's not much chance they'll treat customers as royalty. In companies like Nordstrom, Saturn, Starbucks Coffee, Southwest Airlines, and Hewlett-Packard, you can find people working with joy at something they value. It's more than a paycheck. They work for meaning as well as money. In many cases, they enjoy time at work as much as time doing anything else. Not everyone, and not all the time. But enough to show that it really is possible for a company to be guided more by values and vision than rules and commands.

Those companies, and others like them, recognize a deeper truth: Our life is governed by symbols. What is sometimes viewed as mere fluff is the real stuff of life. We die for flags or philosophies. We live through heroes or heroines. We celebrate seasons with special holidays—Thanksgiving, Christmas or Chanukah, Easter or Sadu, the Fourth of July, or just a summer picnic. The cycle never ends—seasonal events repeat themselves through time. We celebrate triumph with festival and frolic. We cope with tragedy through solemn pomp and circumstance. The death of Princess Diana set the stage for ritual and ceremony that eclipsed in grandeur and emotion even her widely heralded marriage to Prince Charles. Through storytelling, life's lessons and lore seep through our pores and lodge in our hearts and souls. All this is the stuff of culture. Without it, our lives lose meaning, and we become less human.

FRANK 'N' HOPE: *WHAT'S IT ALL ABOUT, ALFIE?*

Frank:	If you buy that stuff about values and joining hands, I'll give you a good price on a bridge.
Hope:	You think it's all B.S.
Frank:	I know it is.
Hope:	Is it B.S. in your family too?
Frank:	No comparison. At home, it's my show. Here, they give me a bit part in a bad play.
Hope:	No hope for anything better?
Frank:	Why flog a dead horse? You survive, you get a paycheck. That's the deal.
Hope:	If you buy that deal, maybe I can sell *you* a bridge. Why spend your life in a lousy show?

The same is true of life at work. Lots of cynics paint vivid portraits of work stripped of meaning and purpose. They'll tell you it's all smoke, mirrors, and manipulation. They'll respond with sarcasm and guffaws if you try to tell them that work doesn't have to be that way. They're deeply skeptical about stories of companies that unite people around shared values and bring excitement, meaning and purpose to life on the job. But such places exist—and you can help to create them. Places where you can join hands, cry, and grieve with your colleagues. Where stories are told and retold, to carry the legacy forward. It won't work if it's only management manipulation. It has to be something people create together to give the workplace oomph and pizzazz.

What can you do if you're locked in a sterile or toxic workplace like the one in Figure 10-1? You could always

Figure 10-1. Some cultures are more toxic than others.

leave and look for a better situation. Alternatives exist, and they're often looking for people who want to help build a more positive work environment. Another possibility is to look for others who are bored, pissed off, and tired of a Monday through Friday moratorium on life. You might have the makings of one of the cabals discussed in Chapter 9. Together, germs create disease, and disease is contagious when defenses are down. Workplaces are filled with grassroots initiatives that have made them better places to work, but we rarely hear about them. Blemishes, failures, foibles, and stupidity get most of the media attention. We hear about the bad and bizarre, and it's comforting to think that others have it even worse than we do. But it doesn't satisfy our craving for something bigger or better. Do yourself and your coworkers a favor. There are steps you can take as a manager, and others you can take regardless of where you fall in the pecking order.

FRANK 'N' HOPE: *TOO LATE?*

Hope: Sometimes I wonder if I should get out myself. Is it too late?

Frank: We're both stuck. But at least I've learned the ropes and know my way around.

Hope: That's because you've been here so long. This place is hard to read, and you don't get much help.

Frank: Too tough for you? Welcome to the real world. Sink or swim.

Hope: Maybe we could row together?

Frank: No one's ever offered.

WHAT MANAGERS CAN DO

If you're a manager, there's much you can do to infuse your operation with passion and purpose. You can learn from examples like Herb Kelleher, who made Southwest Airlines exemplify how play and profit can go hand in hand. Or Mary Kay Ashe of Mary Kay Cosmetics, who showed how celebration enhances self-esteem and fuels energy that bolsters the bottom line. Too many managers are convinced that rationality and toughness are the keys to success: Be lean and mean, drive your employees to greater efforts. Yet this strategy rarely works in the long term. As noted earlier, the logic of "beatings will continue until morale improves" eventually destroys productivity as well as spirit.

As a boss, weigh the options carefully. If you conform to the old norms, you may delude yourself into thinking you're a great success looking for a place to happen, if you could only find subordinates half as bright as you. The other option is to take risks and try something outside the envelope. Get people together to figure out what your operation really stands for and cares about. Anoint and celebrate people whose good deeds stand out. Hold a corporate event. Take your group on a rafting expedition or a ropes course. Get people together to share stories. Sure, it will feel risky, and there will be skeptics. But if employees respond and begin to get energized by new possibilities, you can't be that far off the mark.

GRASSROOTS INITIATIVES

You don't have to be in charge to lead the charge. People create culture. Once created, it starts to shape them. One of the greatest catalysts in the workplace petri dish is leadership. You have a choice as an employee, manager, or executive. You can be an eternal victim or scapegoat of the cultural status quo, or you can step out, step up, and shape the way things get done. You could fail or get fired. But at least you'll have a few great stories to tell—and you'll probably land a better job someplace else. That's what the evidence tells us. But you're going to have to believe it, and believe in yourself, in order to move ahead. What are some possible first steps?

1. *Publish your own broadside.* We know a group of people with enough local talent to start their own comic strip.

They filled it with caricatures of employees and managers. It's almost as funny as Dilbert and has a secondary benefit. It gets some issues out there for people to work on as well as laugh at. Another friend, a cubicle-dweller in a big bank, started putting out his own weekly newsletter with irreverent accounts of the week's highlights. He E-mailed it to a few close friends at first. But the word got out, and pretty soon everyone in the office wanted a subscription.

2. *Set aside some time for storytelling.* Everyone loves a good story. And every workplace generates lots of them. The trouble is they're rarely shared in a public forum. An organization we know convenes a storytelling festival twice a year. They call it the semiannual "Pits and Berries" hour. Stories about the bad times—the "pits"—share equal attention with the good times—the "berries." An applause meter decides the winning Pit or Berry. It's two hours chock-full of both sidesplitting and heartwarming tales. In another example, an aerospace company was troubled by a wide chasm between two distinct subcultures. One consisted of old-timers who fondly remembered an earlier boom period. The other group contained newcomers who had entered a shrinking company in leaner times. Each group had its own sense of history, values, and folkways. At a corporate retreat, an elder storyteller was persuaded to hold forth after dinner. His fellow veterans enjoyed hearing the stories again. In hearing them for the first time, the newcomers developed a deeper appreciation of why their senior colleagues felt as they did. Some common threads were created to connect the two groups.

3. *Create special parentheses in the workday.* In a less hectic, pressured world, it used to be easier to set aside informal time for people to bond and relate to each other in expressive outlets such as coffee breaks, potluck lunches, or shared time

at the local watering hole on Fridays. The speed-up of modern life has often reduced these refreshing pauses to the vanishing point. Yet they're vital opportunities for people to chew and chat and develop relationships that cut across levels and functions. Just spending time with colleagues at breakfast, or lunch, or a late afternoon drink can foster dialogue and create common bonds that are hard to form during the regular workday. But even purely functional activities can take on ritual meaning. The slides and presentations at a meeting. The traditional scrub before surgery. The first officer's walk around an aircraft before take-off. Roll call for police officers before they go on duty. These activities achieve task objectives *and* provide opportunities for bonding and strengthening cultural values.

4. *Celebrate.* There's always something to celebrate at work—people's birthdays or promotions, company anniversaries and milestones. A lot of companies draw on the seasons—holiday parties, summer picnics, Halloween, or spring festivals. Recognizing individual accomplishment provides another good excuse for a party, as do collective triumphs—a new product, a great year, or landing a big customer. But workplace disappointments need ceremonies too. One large U.S. retail firm recently gathered employees together and turned the spotlight on some recent screw-ups. Everyone got a good laugh. The bosses' message to the troops: "Here we learn from our mistakes." On the occasion of the company's tenth anniversary, employees were transported to Hawaii for a major extravaganza. A big hit at the time, it produced many long-term residual benefits.

5. *Create theater.* Theater lets people express things that are hard to say directly in meetings or through the usual channels. The stage blends fact and fiction, seriousness and

humor, work and play. Regular occasions for skits and other dramatic episodes give employees and managers a fun-filled forum for learning and resolving issues that are otherwise hard to tackle. A medical center we know annually creates a stage. Any employee, group, or manager can sign up to do a musical number, a skit, or a rap. Issues are aired. People get their points across. Employees vent, and management learns. They call the activity "theater therapy." In another company, the annual national sales meeting always opens with a homemade video produced by staff at headquarters. One year, the tape opened with the president, looking serious and sounding solemn, introducing what he pitches as a major new initiative. It sounds like it might be pretty important, until you learn that it involves a new corporate dress code: nudity. The many benefits of the new program (less time worrying about what to wear, visitors to headquarters are much friendlier, etc.) are touted by a series of employees, all nude except for judiciously placed typewriters, flowers, or file drawers. It's a tape you have to see to appreciate, but, needless to say, it brought down the house.

There are many other ways to invigorate life at work and create a culture that pulls people together rather than splits them apart. All it takes is a little initiative. Don't wait for the boss to act—or, if you're in charge, support the initiatives and creativity that come from the ranks. It'll work.

WORK AS A CALLING

The arrival of a new millennium coincides with a time of enormous social and economic transition. As in other similar eras, we're seeing a great upsurge in attention to basic questions about the meaning of work and life. For much of the late twentieth century, many of us had put these questions aside and relied on the twin faiths of technology and consumerism. More money meant more stuff, and more stuff brought greater happiness. Or so we thought. More and more people, among them the most talented and successful, are having serious second thoughts. They're realizing that they want their life to mean more than a big house and lots of expensive toys. Increasingly they're saying to employers, "What's the purpose here? Why is this work worth doing?"

Progressive companies see this trend, and they're starting to respond. Take Cerner Corporation, a producer of software for the health-care industry. Every new Cerner associate attends an orientation program. First item on the agenda is a videotape—a moving tale from a cancer patient about the run-around she experiences every time she has to visit another doctor or hospital unit. Always a clipboard with more forms to fill out, all asking for the same information. Always having to go back over the same questions that she's answered over and over. Cerner's message to its employees is simple: We hired you for something more important than producing software. You're here to improve lives by reducing stress, frustration, and anxiety for patients like the woman in the video.

You can minimize the meaning and purpose in any work by putting the words "just" or "only" in front of it. "I just crank out code." "I'm only a teacher." Listen carefully, and you'll hear lots of people talk that way. It's true that some kinds of work are intrinsically easier to justify than others. Cerner has an easier job explaining its purpose than companies that market cigarettes or child pornography. Such exceptions aside, most work makes a difference, or it wouldn't be done for long. It's a matter of looking beyond the daily routine to the bigger picture, the larger good. Who do we serve? What do we offer them? If your workplace doesn't do a very good job of responding to such questions, take some initiative. Start a conversation with coworkers. You might be surprised at what you discover.

ESCAPING CLUELESSNESS X: MAKING WORK MEANINGFUL—AND FUN

- LOTS OF WORKPLACES ARE STERILE OR TOXIC (RESTRUCTURING AND DOWNSIZING OFTEN MAKES THINGS EVEN WORSE)—BUT THEY DON'T HAVE TO BE.
- STORIES, CELEBRATIONS, SHARED VALUES, AND THEATER ALL HELP TO BUILD ROBUST CULTURE.
- ANYONE CAN GET IN ON THE ACT TO BRING MORE FUN AND MEANING TO WORK.

Looking Ahead

- Culture and core values will be increasingly recognized as the vital social glue that infuses an organization with passion and purpose.
- Workers will increasingly demand more than a paycheck. They'll want to know the higher calling or ennobling purpose of their work.

SUGGESTIONS FOR FURTHER READING

Ed Schein's *Organization Culture and Leadership* offers an in-depth look at cultural assumptions. In *Corporate Cultures,* Terry Deal and Allan Kennedy offer a framework for analyzing cultural patterns. Their work is updated in *The New Corporate Cultures.*

See the Biliography for publication details of these books.

PART VI

CHANGE, LEADERSHIP, AND SPIRIT

Cope with change

Learn to lead

Find your path

START:
Know what you want
Create conspiracy
Part the waters
Clarify new jobs
Expect conflict
Celebrate past, future
Choose a path
Fog
Bog
Piracy
Service

11

Understanding Change and Leadership: Rotating Tires or Fixing Flats?

If you work in a place that's been sterile, toxic or unproductive for as long as anyone can remember, what's the chance things will ever get better? Do organizations ever really change? You've seen lots of big, new programs that stirred everything up for a while before disappearing without a trace. You've heard fashionable managerial talk about change and transformation. Reengineering? Customer focus? Cultural transformation? Total quality? Empowerment? High-performing organizations? We've heard them all. Plenty of ideas. But how many ever become reality? Still, productive change isn't an impossible dream. You can help it happen by leading from where you are.

Dilbert's digs probably won't improve in the near future. Not if Scott Adams is smart. His cutting edge needs a screwed-up situation as a foil. If he created a workplace of vision and virtue, he'd lose most of his readers. In one strip, for example, Adams lampoons management's love affair with reorganizing. Wally asks how the latest restructuring is supposed to sharpen focus on the core business. Has the core business changed, Wally wonders, or is it just that every previous reorganization was a failure? The boss responds by asking what Wally does when his car has a flat tire. "Well, if I'm you," Wally replies, "I rotate the tires."

If you look at the track record, the likelihood of dramatic change in a typical workplace is pretty bleak. Many proposed changes end up perpetuating the status quo. Others do more harm than good. Ambitious managers fall from grace a lot faster than anyone expected. "Same old, same old," as they say. If you find it hard to recall a recent change initiative that fizzled, you may just be in denial. Failure is disappointing and leaves a residual sting. We'd just as soon put it behind us.

No human group easily escapes the remarkable staying power of old ways. Check out America's progress on converting to the metric system of weights and measurements. The government decided in the 1950s to replace pounds and quarts with kilos and liters. The rationale? Most of the world operates on the metric system. As business becomes more global, being out of step creates even more confusion and hinders trade. Like the American carmakers whose early efforts to crack the Japanese market went nowhere because they didn't bother to put the steering wheels on the right side of the car. So there were persuasive arguments for bringing our standards into line with the rest of the world.

Globalization spread even faster and farther than anyone anticipated forty years ago. But what's sensible doesn't always fly. We're wed to old ways and don't give them up easily. In the United States, we still buy gas by the gallon, meat by the pound, and wine by the fifth. Speed limits are still in miles per hour. Sure, American speedometers show kilometers (in small print), but who pays attention? Such inattention had disastrous results for the Mars Climate Orbiter. The satellite was off course and crashed. Why? One group of scientists did their calculations in metrics, while the other group was using the English system. Millions of dollars were wasted, and it was a black eye for the U.S. space program.

It's the same sort of thing in the world of work. Changes that are important, even vital, for success and survival die in infancy. Why? One obvious reason is that too many changes are hatched at the top and imposed on everyone else by top dogs who assume they alone have good ideas. The boss goes to a conference or reads an article in *Fortune* or the *Harvard Business Review*. Presto, this is exactly what we need to do. Later on, the boss tries to figure out why such a brilliant brainstorm never got on track.

When it comes to change in the workplace, we're all pretty much at sea. Bosses and employees alike scratch their heads and echo the words of Butch Cassidy and the Sundance Kid as they marveled at the staying power of a persistent posse on their trail: "Who are those guys?" It turns out that those "guys" are us and people like us who can't quite fathom the mysteries of change.

FRANK 'N' HOPE: *A 100 PERCENT FAILURE RATE*

Frank: I hear you're on one of the "World Class Teams."

Hope: True. We start next week.

Frank: Waste of time.

Hope: You're writing us off before we start?

Frank: Our failure rate is 100%. You should've seen all the other fiascos. Like in the '70s when we were all going to fly with Jonathan Livingston Seagull. The only thing that came out of it was jokes about bird poop.

Hope: That's ancient history.

Frank: The parade never stops. The leadership program where we went out to the woods and got lost. The ropes course where the boss broke his leg. The total quality program that was a total bust. I could go on all day.

Hope: How long is the business gonna go on if we can't compete?

Frank: For starters, fire the consultants. Then kill all the silly meetings. We might get a lot more done.

WHY CHANGE FAILS

Change is so tough because it kicks up a set of barriers that are as reliable as a Swiss watch. Unless those barriers are recognized and resolved—which they usually aren't—failure is almost a sure thing. Here's a list of the most important obstacles:

1. *Change breeds anxiety and incompetence.* Take a simple example that might be familiar. Suppose that you brought home a personal computer a few years back. Imagine that it came with a software package named Max. Max was supposed to process your words, or crunch your numbers, or balance your checkbook. At first, Max drove you crazy. He seemed like the brainchild of idiot-sadists who deliberately made him as unfriendly as possible. After a lot of trial and error—endless frustration with a manual that might as well have been written in Old Church Slavonic, and hours on hold with a so-called tech support line—you finally got Max to do some work. Gradually, you even got used to his personality quirks. Eventually Max evolved into an old friend. You'd learned to get along. You even survived the upgrade to Max 2.0. Then, tragedy struck. Max was orphaned—his parent company was knocked out of the market by an adroit competitor. By now, you and Max were pretty much married, and you were in no mood for a divorce. But things were changing pretty fast in the computer biz, and Max was frozen in the past. The relationship was turning sour. You had to keep up with the times, and Max was lagging.

So what happens if you abandon Max and take up with a totally new software package, Sheila 1.0? First off, you'd feel incompetent. The skills you'd mastered over several years would suddenly become obsolete. You'd find yourself continually annoyed and sometimes furious because everything that was easy with Max seems impossible with Sheila. Naturally, you'd be reluctant and resistant. Who wants to feel bungling and edgy? Why volunteer to be in a situation where you're tearing your hair, screaming profanities, or breaking down in tears as you try to get a complete stranger to work as well as Max did?

It's the same thing in the workplace for almost any innovation. People wonder if they'll ever get up to speed. They worry about being left in the dust. A popular example in recent years has been the adoption of "enterprise resource planning": gigantic computer programs that are supposed to track just about everything companywide. In early 1996, Brother Industries in Memphis figured that eight months would be plenty of time to get everyone up to speed on their big, new system. A year later they brought in a new chief information officer to clean up the mess. His take on the situation he encountered: "They figure, it's packaged software, they didn't have to train anyone—four information systems folks could easily teach 250 users how to run it. Everything that could go wrong did."*

2. *Change disrupts established patterns.* A second predictable problem with any change effort is easy to see if you think about it for a minute. Like families, every workplace evolves basic understandings of who does what and who has the final say. In a well-oiled machine, the gears mesh; roles and relationships are synchronized to assure predictable outcomes. When any role changes, everything else gets out of sync. Think about when you, or your kid, went off to college for the first time. Thanksgiving vacation rolls around and you're all back together for the holidays. The traditional dinner goes off according to custom. After dinner, the following conversation plays out:

*Quoted in Claudia H. Deutsch, "Software That Can Make a Grown Company Cry," *The New York Times*, November 8, 1998, pp. 3–13.

FRESHMAN (casually): I'm going out to see some friends.
PARENT: Well . . . O.K. Be home by eleven.
FRESHMAN (quickly and firmly): Get a life, folks! I set my own ground rules now.

Similar encounters are a staple of workplace change. New technology gives employees access to more information, and managers struggle to maintain control. Joe figures out a shortcut for speeding up the work, and Shawna has trouble adjusting to the new tempo. A reengineering effort overhauls operations without corresponding adjustments in marketing. In Brother Industries's troubled implementation of enterprise computing, the snags caused by inadequate training were compounded by massive role confusion. The project team that designed the software was made up mostly of computer nerds. Many of their assumptions about user needs were far off the mark. The result, said one executive, "was a real case of garbage in, garbage out."* Inventory and production problems skyrocketed because the system provided the wrong data, or users couldn't figure out how to get at the data that was buried in there somewhere. A well-established structure can ensure predictability, coordination, and a well-controlled environment. Change undermines all that, creating confusion, chaos, and a widespread fear of being out of control.

3. *Change produces warfare, winners, and losers.* Even if you can figure out how to overcome incompetence and confusion, workplace change summons another formidable demon: politics. Machiavelli observed approximately 500 years ago that those who stand to lose power in the new

*Ibid.

order of things will organize in staunch opposition, while those who might benefit offer only lukewarm support. So it goes with anything new. People choose sides, and the battle begins. Too often it's a disorderly battle that degenerates into a below-the-belt, back-alley street fight where anything goes. People get hurt and relationships suffer permanent damage. Odds are that the champions of the status quo outlast the proponents of the new order. Change fragments the workplace into allies, opponents, and fence-sitters. On most balance sheets the opponents of change are heavy favorites.

4. *Change means loss.* Even deeper below the surface lurks another powerful dynamic that's basic to being human. Just as we bond with old T-shirts and treasured mementos, we form attachments to well-entrenched traditions and ways. They may not be working; they may even be counterproductive. But they're the devil we know. The attachments are rooted much more in sentiment than reason. We're all pretty sentimental when it comes to symbols, objects, or activities that have real meaning to us. If you're old enough, you remember the caboose on the end of a train. Years ago you could wave at the crew as the train went by. Now, the caboose is gone, replaced by an electronic device attached to the last car. It handles the function just as well, at a fraction of the cost. What's the problem? Memories and how you felt—how you'd also like your kids to feel. It was once a cross-generational bond. No longer. The bottom line: We're all for change as long as we don't lose anything we care about and don't have to do anything too differently. The human race is held together by common rituals, symbols, and traditions. Change unravels the fabric that holds us together and gives meaning to life at work.

MAKING CHANGE WORK: LEAD FROM WHERE YOU ARE

How can you and others respond to change, or even initiate it, without ending up on the rocks? The key here is the familiar L word: leadership. Leadership is about change, and about finding ways for people to work together to find and solve problems. Tons of books and articles about leadership have flowed off the presses in recent years. Some of it is pretty good. But almost all of it starts with a misleading assumption: You're already in charge of something—you're the CEO, or you run some big chunk of the company, or at least you're in charge of some group or unit. But, contrary to a widely held assumption, you don't have to be in charge to be a leader. Sure, being in a highly visible and powerful role gives you some advantages: People pay attention to what you say and usually try to please you. But it's also true that when you're high up, people pressure you to keep things safe, stable, and predictable. They want you to take them to a safe haven, not embark on some high-risk adventure. That makes it harder to lead, because change always makes things risky and confusing for a while. The truth is, too many folks with big titles and fancy offices couldn't lead starving teenagers to a hamburger stand.

Leading from anywhere is easier if we get past the media-driven assumption that leadership only comes from superheroes—powerful, charismatic, larger-than-life champions who single-handedly destroy monsters, overturn tyrants, and clean up whole towns while awed onlookers watch from a safe distance. Nothing could be further from the truth. Leadership isn't about position or solo heroics. It's about working with people to help them figure out where they want to go, how they can get there, and how they can summon the courage to move ahead. This means that leadership is always a relationship built on two-way communication. Leadership certainly requires the ability to influence others, but listening is just as important as giving directions or issuing commands. You can't lead without followers, and people will follow willingly only if they feel they'll be better off going along with you.

It's easier to lead if you're in a crisis situation, when everyone agrees that things are terrible and something has to be done. Like the situation Gordon Bethune found when he took over Continental Airlines. Nowhere to go but up—or out of business. But suppose you're in a situation that's more like slow death or water torture than an immediate catastrophe. Regardless of your starting point, change and leadership are never easy. But they're always possible. Try the seven steps of our escape-from-cluelessness-lead-from-anywhere model. Our lawyers, if we had any, would want us to disclaim any warranty against consequential damages. That said, these are time-tested strategies that are a helluva lot better than flying blind. And they can work for anybody: the CEO or the guy who drives her limo, the plant manager or a worker on the assembly line, the school superintendent or the classroom teacher.

1. *Know what you want.* To lead, you need a goal or vision: a mental image or picture of what you want or where you really want to go. Exercise your imagination. Talk to your spouse, friends, or colleagues. Think about what would make you excited to come to work. A meaningful job? Close colleagues? Producing something you can be proud of? Then ask what would need to change to get you to a better place. What specific changes would move you in the right direc-

tion? When your picture of what you want gets clearer, you're ready for step 2.

2. *Create a conspiracy: Share your dreams and enlist others' support.* Dreams and visions take off when you get others on board. You do this over time in a series of get-togethers, some one-on-one, some in groups. It can be over coffee and doughnuts in the morning, at coffee breaks, lunch time in the cafeteria, or after work at the local pub. Persistence and involvement are the keys. Lay it on the line and see what happens. You might be pleasantly surprised to discover that others want some of the same things you do. They're just as frustrated as you are and are even willing to join you in an effort to turn things around. It's surprising how much energy is wasted by fretting, grumbling, and longing for a better life at work. Life in your individual silo can be pretty lonely. Converting impotent moaning into a local conspiracy opens up the potential for a more exciting and engaging game.

Once the conspiracy begins to take off, you need a strategy for getting past the predictable barriers to change. Stop in at each of the checkpoints in the next four steps. Maybe not in the order we've listed them, because every change effort plays differently. But make sure you attend to all four.

3. *Part the waters to smooth the passage.* Change scares people for all the reasons we discussed earlier. To overcome their fears, they need time to adapt, support during the transition, and opportunities to learn new knowledge and skills. Develop a realistic timetable. It takes about nine months from conception until a baby is ready to be born, and rushing the process is a bad idea. The bigger and more dramatic the change, the more time people need to make adjustments. They also need support: someone to talk to about their struggles, a coach to help them over the rough spots, a friend to

join them on the journey. They need opportunities to master the understanding and skills that the new ways demand. With time and support, on-the-job learning is sometimes enough. Major change requires more: some form of targeted training program.

A big accounting firm wanted to change its professionals from traffic cops to consultants. Traditionally, when clients asked, "Can I do this?" the accountants answered "Yes, you can," or "No, you can't." In the new approach, their job was to ask questions and find out what was behind the question. Then they could work with the client to develop a solution or refer the client to someone else. It sounds simple enough, but it was a big shift in mind-set and habits. A training program was developed bottom-up and then critiqued by senior partners. It got people up to speed with new skills and provided a psychological support group, since everyone was in pretty much the same boat.

Scott Adams occasionally sends Dilbert to an off-site training, typically involving a cynical lecture on corporate ethics or walking in bare feet on hot coals. But Adams's view is colored by his recollection of the time a former employer sent him off to a ropes course. A coworker who was supposed to break his fall in a trust exercise stepped aside and let him crash to the ground. Bad training is a big waste of time and money, but good training is possible and usually essential for effective change. Typically, it's developed in-house by people who are close to the situation and know the skills needed for the new program to fly.

4. *Make sure people know their new jobs.* If things seem confused now in your company, wait until you introduce something new. Make sure people discuss and negotiate the emerging nuts and bolts of who does what and how people relate to one another. That goes a long way toward realigning

roles and relationships so people's efforts mesh, not clash. A memo to all hands announcing new assignments just won't cut it. Imposing a new structure on people without dialogue is a sure-fire recipe for a full-fledged free fall.

In the early 1990s, the city of Chicago tried to revitalize its ailing public schools with a dramatic program of decentralization. The hope was to cut down on bureaucracy and red tape stifling the schools. Put a local school council in charge of each building. Give them power to hire and fire the principal. Let neighborhoods run their own schools. Who cares more about a school than the people who live near it? A year later, evaluators went in to see how it was going. Their findings weren't pretty:

> During 1990–91 there was substantial confusion among people at all levels of this system about what was meant by reform, who was responsible for what elements of reform, and whether or not their actions and the actions of others were effective in achieving the goals of reform. Our judgment is that this confusion continues into the present. . . . The actual outcomes and indicators of reform fall far short of the target levels established in the plan.*

Almost everyone involved in the decentralization effort found themselves in unfamiliar roles and circumstances. But there was no training and almost no help as they struggled to cut through the confusion and figure out what they were supposed to do. People needed new skills, and they needed help figuring out how to work together. Watch a team of

*D. William Quinn, Monica Stewart, and Jeri Nowakowski, "An External Evaluation of Systemwide School Reform in Chicago," *International Journal of Educational Reform,* January 1993, p. 8.

six-year-olds play soccer. You see a moving herd clumped around the ball. No one has a clue about passing or playing a position. That's about how it was on a lot of local school councils. Come back and watch those six-year-old soccer players when they get to be eight or nine. It's still not World Cup play, but they know their assignments and they're starting to anticipate what their teammates will do. It took time, coaching, and practice. Those are all vital to success. It's the same with change anywhere.

5. *Expect conflict, bring it into the open, and negotiate.* We'll give you an ironclad guarantee that changes will generate conflict as soon as they move from abstraction to action. People don't hand over power willingly. When they see their special interests and turf being gored, they figure out ways to strike back. Usually not in broad daylight or public view. They form coalitions to resist the change and find countless opportunities behind the scenes and under wraps to slow things down and screw them up. People spend so much time protecting their turf or conspiring to dust off someone else that performance quickly starts to fall off. For example, the merger between Northwest and Republic Airlines produced conflict everywhere. One that had a direct impact on customer service was animosity among the flight attendants. Republic attendants traditionally had better hotel accommodations and fewer duties than was customary at Northwest. When the two groups tried to work together, Northwest attendants soon came to view their Republic counterparts as spoiled princesses. In turn, Republic flight attendants labeled their new colleagues "Stepford wives," after the Hollywood film about a group of robotized women. The political battles were legendary. For customers, it meant many months when it was worth going out of one's way to fly some other airline.

Say you're a cubicle dweller and suddenly you notice

new faces appearing in the office suite. You can become paranoid and rally your forces to formulate a battle strategy. The resulting war is rarely very productive. It's like a battle between guards and forwards on the same basketball team: Everyone loses. If you expect conflict, and understand that it's a natural part of a change process, you're less likely to be thrown by it. Instead of saying, "Oh, no, this is terrible," you just say, "This is normal. Let's find ways to deal with it." Then you bring the issues to the table to see what can be worked out. It's called negotiation—the process of give-and-take between people who have different ideas and interests, but still have to work together. It works best in "arenas"—places where differences can be aired in the presence of rules, referees, rounds, and spectators. In the accounting firm mentioned earlier, both allies and opponents of the change were invited to the training sessions. The stage was set for a lively encounter. The exchanges were intense and heated. But the fight was fair, and the back-and-forth forum yielded a new approach that most people could support.

6. *Celebrate the past and look forward to the future with farewell parties, funerals, and wakes.* The final powerful barrier to change is our innate human desire to build meaning around important symbols and symbolic activity. When we lose our attachments to these existential anchors, we experience a deep sense of loss. Shortly after the Northwest/Republic merger, management sent crews out to repaint all of Republic's planes, replacing Republic's goose with Northwest's solid red tail. The company learned a powerful lesson the hard way. Symbols are powerful. It cuts deep when you mess around with them. Another dramatic example of this dynamic surfaced in the wake of AT&T's 1982 divestiture of its local telephone companies. It became apparent very quickly that "Ma Bell" was more than an abstraction. She repre-

sented 100 years of universal service delivered by generations of Bell employees. Soon after the divestiture was announced, reports of psychological problems, drug and alcohol abuse, divorces, and even suicides started to circulate widely. In a formal company questionnaire, a question about the impact of the change on employees' personal lives opened the gates for an outpouring of loss, hurt, and grief. It was then that CEO Charlie Brown reportedly said, "We've got to do something."

Meanwhile, out in the operating companies, the troops were taking things into their own hands. Many found themselves plunged into the complex pool of emotions that accompany loss—anger, denial, sadness, ambivalence. Once they understood the deeper issues, they saw the need for wakes, funerals, mourning periods, and companions to help them let go, heal, and move on. In many companies today, both cubicle workers and bosses are convening some fantastic transition rituals. Doesn't take a lot of money or effort. And everyone knows how to design and participate in such an event.

7. *Aim for greatness: focus, passion, wisdom, and courage.* A lot has been written about the qualities of good leaders. Some argue there's one best way to lead. Others say that it all depends. It's actually some of both. You don't need to have a certain personality or a particular leadership style. You don't have to be tall, or male, or extroverted. Yet certain qualities seem to turn up wherever you find outstanding leadership.

The first is *focus*: a clear sense of where you're trying to go. A central challenge of leadership, as our friend Allan Kennedy once reported, is "how to get the whole herd moving roughly west." Getting the herd moving is tough enough, but the bigger problem is figuring out which way is west. A new school principal once consulted us about his opening speech to his faculty for the first day of school. He proudly shared his list of twenty-one key priorities. He seemed crestfallen when we gently suggested two or three priorities was plenty. Ronald Reagan ran a very focused presidency: reduce taxes and maintain American strength abroad. People could agree or disagree about his priorities, but everyone was pretty clear about where he wanted to go. His successor, George Bush, was more like our friend the young principal. Bush wanted to improve the schools, strengthen the economy, fight the Gulf War, improve the environment, and many more. A major reason Bush lost his bid for reelection was that people had trouble figuring out what he stood for.

A second quality of great leadership is *passion*: a deep personal and emotional commitment to the work, the people, and the place. You can't fake passion: It's rooted in loving what you do and the people you work with. Passion is contagious. People are a lot more likely to get behind a leader who demonstrates deep commitment and a willingness to do whatever it takes.

A third characteristic of great leadership is *wisdom:* the ability to understand that things are complicated without becoming immobilized. Some very smart people can't lead because they can't get past, "On the one hand, we could go west, but on the other hand, we could go north, or maybe east. . . ." Then there are leaders who aren't smart enough to understand the complexity of the situation. They're the tunnel-vision zealots who take groups off cliffs or mire them in swamps. Wisdom is something that's only acquired over time and through the hard knocks of experience. It's vital for leadership because it helps you to know what you're up against and to see a clear path ahead.

The final characteristic of great leadership is *courage*. It's always risky to step out ahead of the pack. You have to place a bet against the future—choosing one path among a variety of competing possibilities. Tomorrow is always uncertain. We never have all the information we'd like. It takes courage to choose a course based on your judgment and values. Down the road you might discover that you went down a blind alley or over a precipice. If so, there'll be plenty of critics to rub it in. Even if you're right, there are usually some people who will say you're wrong. All this is what Harry Truman had in mind when he counseled, "If you can't stand the heat, get out of the kitchen." Taking the heat is part of the leader's unwritten job description. But if you know where you're going and you're passionate about getting there, you'll probably find the wisdom and courage to move forward.

Every organization has things that work well. These need frequent celebration. Every organization also has programs, strategies, and people that are past their prime or going downhill. These need comfort and dignity. Every corporate graveyard is full of old horses, old programs, and people who have departed—voluntarily or otherwise. These need burial and a commemorative service. Always emerging are new starts and fresh ideas. These need protection and ample resources. Do it and you'll leave Dilbert's digs in the dust. Change can happen if you rely more on common sense than the latest corporate fad.

ESCAPING CLUELESSNESS XI: COPING WITH CHANGE AND LEARNING TO LEAD

- SOMETIMES WE CHOOSE CHANGE; OFTEN SOMEONE ELSE CHOOSES IT FOR US.
- CHANGE EFFORTS RUN INTO FOUR UNIVERSAL BARRIERS:
  1. INDIVIDUALS' RESISTANCE TO ANXIETY AND FEELING INCOMPETENT
  2. DISRUPTION OF ESTABLISHED PATTERNS
  3. CONFLICT BETWEEN WINNERS AND LOSERS
  4. LOSS
- CHANGE TAKES LEADERSHIP.
- YOU CAN LEAD FROM ANYWHERE IF:
  - YOU KNOW YOUR GOAL.
  - ENLIST OTHERS.
  - PART THE WATERS.
  - MAKE SURE PEOPLE KNOW THEIR JOB.
  - DEAL WITH CONFLICT.
  - CELEBRATE.
  - LEAD WITH FOCUS, PASSION, WISDOM, AND COURAGE.

12

Choosing a Life Path: Fog, Bog, Piracy, or Service?

In previous chapters, we focused on how-to questions: How to survive and thrive amid workplace politics. How to make your job better and more satisfying. How to understand and escape bureaucratic traps, and how to plunge successfully into the depths of organizational culture. In this chapter we shift to even more challenging questions of where and why. Where are you going in your work and life? Why? Will the path you're on take you where you want to go?

We discussed two levels of cluelessness in earlier chapters: personal and situational. Now we address the deepest and most difficult level: spiritual. If the word "spiritual" makes you nervous, you're not alone. But hang in. We're talking Life 101 here: basic questions of where you're headed and what's really important to you. We're not peddling a "New Age" cult or a religion you never heard of. If you have a faith that works for you, keep it, strengthen it, and deepen your commitment. In any event, keep reading.

Along with the change in topic, you'll see a change in tone and style. No more cartoons (sorry). Instead, you'll find poetry and themes from the world's spiritual traditions. They'll help us get closer to issues of heart and spirit that are central in all our lives.

If you look around at your coworkers, friends, and family, you'll probably find that most of them are on one of four life paths that we'll explore. At least one will probably fit your own direction. The first of these paths is shrouded in fog, which makes it hard to see ahead. A second path is a soggy marsh that drags you down. A third is the path of piracy, a mugger's lane that can take you to the top—or get you canceled out. The fourth is the path of service, a challenging spiritual quest traveled by bold seekers looking for a better life and a better world. Now may be a great time to weigh your life's alternatives.

THE FOGGY PATH: WHAT'S IT ALL ABOUT?

You're lost in the fog if you don't really have a direction and haven't figured out what life's all about. It's exemplified in Yogi Berra's comment as he was driving to the Baseball Hall of Fame in Cooperstown, "We're lost, but we're making good time." These days, the foggy path is crowded with people who need a personal navigation system, but can't seem to find one in any of the mail-order catalogues. They're pushed and pulled by whatever pressures or people happen along. They look outside for clues on how to live their inner lives: What are the neighbors doing? What brands are film and sports stars promoting? What does the boss expect? What do the advice columns or magazine ads suggest I should do or care about? What would Martha Stewart or Michael Jordan do?

The tragedy of the foggy path is this: Sooner or later, you look around and wonder how you got where you are. Too often, that produces a crushing realization: You're lost and you've squandered a big chunk of your life. You get depressed. Or bitter. Or you drown your frustrations in booze and pills. A fictional example is singer Sally Bowles, the lead role in the film and play *Cabaret*. It's a good role: Liza Minnelli got an Academy Award for the 1972 film. Natasha Richardson earned a Tony award on Broadway in 1998. Said Richardson of Bowles, "She's lost in the sense that, when she can go left or right, she'll take the wrong turn and chase false values. She's so frightened of responsibility that she becomes a drug addict."*

An everyday, real-life example is Edwin. The son of a preacher, Edwin never found his calling. He came of age during the Depression. After a couple of years of college, the money dried up, and he dropped out. The best job he could land was as a salesman. Edwin had multiple talents: He was a church choir soloist, a strong tennis player, an amateur actor, and a charming raconteur. Selling was OK—he liked people—but his heart was never fully in it. He did it to earn a living and support his family. He gradually did a little better each year. In his early forties, he took a job with a new company. Moved his family halfway across the United States. Bigger house, nice neighborhood. It seemed like a high point in his career. But he'd bet on the wrong horse. The company got in trouble, and the job dissolved. Edwin and his family learned about downsizing long before the word became popular.

*Quoted in G. Buchalter, "Finally, She Could Be Her Own Person," *Parade,* August 9, 1998, p. 4.

After that, Edwin's life slid slowly downhill. He was out of work for a while. When he finally found another job, he took a cut in money and status. The house was sold, and the family reluctantly moved into a two-family rental in still another city. Edwin's sense of humor vanished. He became distant and irritable, relying more and more on alcohol to survive from one day to the next. After a while, everyone around him knew he was a drunk, including his boss. He was finally forced into early retirement, and his wife took a job to support the family. By his sixties, Edwin was a pale remnant of a once-vibrant and confident self. He made occasional attempts to get off the bottle, but never succeeded. When a heart attack killed him at age 70, he was relatively young. But the bigger tragedy was that he had been dying spiritually long before his physical death.

Edwin spent his life on a foggy path. It wasn't a conscious choice. He'd never said to himself, "What the hell, I'll just wander through life without ever thinking about where I'm going or what I really want to do." He did what he felt he had to do to support his family and keep his career on track. When he ran into the midlife storms that few of us avoid, he couldn't cope. One more life of quiet desperation ended tragically.

How do you know if you're in the fog? You're there if your life is chronically disappointing, but you can't figure out why. Or you blame everything on bad luck. You're socked in if you can't answer the "what's it all about?" question. Or if you don't really like your work, or your spouse but can't see another option. You're befogged if your life seems stale and flat, if the only zest and passion you know come secondhand via television or the movies.

If you're in the mist, you need to get moving. In "Passage to India," the poet Walt Whitman had some good advice:

> *Away O soul! Hoist instantly the anchor!*
> *Cut the hawsers—haul out—shake out every sail!*
> *Have we not stood here like trees in the ground long enough?*
> *Have we not grovel'd here long enough, eating and drinking like mere brutes?*
>
> *Sail forth—steer for the deep waters only,*
> *Reckless O soul, exploring, I with thee, and thou with me,*
> *For we are bound where mariner has not yet dared to go,*
> *And we will risk the ship, ourselves, and all.*

Whitman's meaning is pretty clear. Don't just grovel in the face of life. Explore. If the path you're on isn't working, look for another—no doubt one with risk, but with depth as well. Go where you haven't been. Not recklessly or foolishly. You don't want a shipwreck. But keep moving. Look for ways to bring more zest and passion to your work. If you're in a dead-end job or the wrong career, look for something better. If you've neglected your children or drifted away from your spouse, start turning that around. If liquor or drugs are playing too big a role in your life, get help. Or maybe you just need to turn off the TV and do something more creative and interesting with your free time. There are lots of projects and organizations in your community that could make very good use of your energy and talent. If you've wandered away from your faith, consider a reunion. Or look for a new congregation. No one else can find the path that's right for you. You'll need to get out and look for it. Take Whitman's advice. Don't get stuck like a ship becalmed in a fog. Explore. And steer for the deep water.

THE BOGGY PATH: "THAT'S JUST THE WAY IT IS"

In a fog, it's hard to see ahead. In a bog, it's hard to move forward. You're sucked down at every step. The modern world's crushing pace, relentless pressures, and mind-numbing complexity can easily mire you in your own personal swamp. You may know where you want to go, but can't figure out how to get there. You're too overwhelmed and exhausted from mucking through the mire just trying to cope with each's days challenges and problems. You see no option but to keep slogging. As one Canadian manager put it in an article in *Canadian Business,* "I don't know how to handle it. I don't eat right. I don't sleep. I don't exercise. . . . Business is extremely competitive, and you've got to be prepared to be at it twenty-four hours a day. I'm not saying it's right. I'm not saying it's healthy. I'm saying that's just the way it is."*

Our friend Anne is caught in the same bind. She feels chronically bogged down and, too often, dispirited by perpetual overload. Her husband is a talented, highly productive workaholic who generally leaves home early and comes back late, except when he's out of town. Like many mothers, Anne has primary responsibility for raising the children. They're all in school, but they're sick a lot, so Anne is continually hauling one child or another off to a doctor or an emergency room. Meanwhile, she's trying to hold down a more than full-time job whose pressures and demands often seem to exceed the rewards. In her spare time, she's active in her community and works hard to keep her house and lawn beautiful. She'd like to cook wonderful family meals as her

*Tamsen Tillson, "Is Your Career Killing You?" *Canadian Business,* September 26, 1997, p. 78.

mother did, but more often finds dinner at a fast-food, drive-in window. Anne flops into bed late at night, only to rise early the next day to walk the dog and get a head start on the day's new chores.

Both Anne and the Canadian manager know they *should* find a different path. Even more, they *want* to. But how? The available options seem to offer too little or demand too much. Prioritize and manage time, they've heard again and again. They read books, attend seminars, and buy fancy date-books or computer software. Sometimes, they feel they've become a bit better at delegating, prioritizing, and ignoring the trivia. Yes, the big picture rarely changes. Even their successes often have unintended consequences. One seeker noted that her efforts at improved time management made her more efficient, at the cost of draining too much joy out of life: "In my efforts to take control of my life, I minimized the serendipity from which new friendships and little miracles occur."*

Another widely promoted remedy is simplifying life: Get off the consumer treadmill, tear up the credit cards, live in a smaller house, keep cars for ten years instead of three, cancel all magazines, and eat more meals at home. Many of us have tried for simplicity, but not so many have found it. Maybe we manage to spend a little less and get our debts down. But the kids still need braces and college tuition, and simplicity doesn't seem quite as easy as it's cracked up to be. Other experts urge us to reduce stress and turmoil by exercising, meditating, praying, going on religious retreats, or just walking in the park. All sound things, but too often they become additional chores, compounding the overload and competing with all the other priorities in time-starved lives.

*Quoted from Paula Caproni, "Work/Life Balance: You Can't Get There From Here," *Journal of Applied Behavioral Science,* 33(1), 1997, p. 49.

Better time management, simplification, and stress reduction all have significant potential. But not if they're used like aspirin as just symptom-relief. It's like rearranging deck chairs on a sinking ship: The deck may look more orderly, but the underlying crisis still festers. We may feel more in control because we're at least doing something. But our frantic efforts skirt deeper issues of soul and human spirit. There are many ways to understand soul. James Hillman, in his book *The Soul's Code: In Search of Character and Calling* (New York: Random House, 1996), writes of it as an acorn, the seed that carries an image of who and what we are called to be and do. You can also understand soul as a bedrock sense of self: a fundamental understanding of who you are, what you care about, and where you're going in your life journey.

The Spanish poet Antonio Machado wrote that the only path in life is the one you make for yourself. When you look back, you see where you've been, but not where you're going. Machado's message is simple, but profound. The path behind is only a fleeting trace. Let go of it. You create the path ahead with each new step. Aim wisely. Anne isn't alone, and her bog is by no means unique. Complexities, overload, and economic pressures are staples of modern life. They're created by forces too large for any individual to resolve. Collectively, we all need to engage the question of what we can do in a world going mad. Meanwhile, we need to focus on our own corner of the craziness. Anne knows she's trying to do too much. But she's got well-rehearsed and convincing arguments for maintaining the status quo. Give up her job? They need the money. Get rid of the dog? Her heart would break. Let the house get dirty? The kids have allergies. Move? More stress and disruption. Prioritize? There are still only twenty-four hours in a day.

We all get bogged down when we don't see any options. But there are almost always more choices. The choices may not be easy to find or follow, but they're there. In his book *Good News for Bad Days* our friend, Father Paul Keenan, describes his own realization of this truth:

> The key that opened the door to my soul for me was the realization that I could make choices and that I had options. Now, that sounds like the silliest thing in the world. [But] as I listened to my own feelings, I realized that over the years, I had developed a lack of confidence in my ability to make choices, and that more often than not I had learned to make decisions based on the strong beliefs of others as to what was right for me. . . . I learned that in order not to feel trapped, I had to stop and ask myself, "What are my options here?" and look for two or three different ways to respond. . . . When we feel trapped, stuck in our lives, the feeling is a cry for help. It is the cry of a soul that is being muffled. When we feel abandoned by others, abandoned by God, often it is our soul crying to be unshackled.*

The way out of the bog is to listen to our muffled cries, to explore within ourselves both our wants and our fears. What images of our own perfection do we cling to, and how do they drag us down? What options do we have? Which might put us on a more promising path?

*Father Paul Keenan, *Good News for Bad Days: Living a Soulful Life* (New York: Warner, 1998), pp. 3–5.

THE PATH OF PIRACY: STRIKE FIRST AND COVER YOUR ASS

A third alternative, popular with cynics and hustlers among us, is piracy: the path of self-interest and plunder. Followers of this route generally see themselves as realists—smarter than the suckers around them. You've heard the cynics' catechism: "might makes right," "it's always dog eat dog," "you can't trust anyone," "look out for number one," "you win in life by dying with the most toys," and so on. This is the self-interested route of the slick politicians we met in Chapter 4. As we said then, this path might lead you to wealth and high position, if your enemies don't torpedo you first. But it's a risky and treacherous route. Bryan Burrough and John Helyar discuss a famous example in their book *Barbarians at the Gate* (New York: Harper, 1990). Ross Johnson made the cover of *Time* as poster boy for corporate greed and insensitivity. Johnson's charm and political skills took him to the top in several companies, even though he seemed gifted more for spending money than making it. He eventually landed the top job at tobacco giant R.J. Reynolds. There he found himself atop a business throwing off more than a billion dollars a year. It was more money than even he could spend, though he gave it his best shot. A new headquarters in Atlanta. A fleet of corporate jets soon tagged as the RJR Air Force. Lavish fees to directors, senior executives, and star athletes (top of the line: golfer Jack Nicklaus at $1 million a year). Johnson was having the time of his life, until Reynolds stock lost a third of its value in the market crash of October 1987. Johnson tried to pull off a management-led buyout, but finished second in a high-stakes shoot-out with some of the biggest guns on Wall Street. He lost both his job and the company.

Chainsaw Al Dunlap (remember him from Chapter 2?) is another exemplar of the pirate's path. Like Johnson, he ascended to the apex of several companies and made hundreds of millions of dollars along the way. But he finally fell on his own sword, fired by Sunbeam's board of directors for failing to deliver. Meanwhile, he suffered another affliction of the pirate's voyage: Even his closest relatives saw him as cold and ruthless. Similar fates befell many of the twentieth century's most notorious dark-path travelers. Adolf Hitler committed suicide as his empire collapsed. Pol Pot died ill and reviled in a dreary rural exile. Joseph Stalin, who demonstrated a cunning combination of ruthlessness and political skill, was despised by his wives, children, and closest associates. After dominating the Soviet Union for three decades, he died suddenly and mysteriously just as he was about to launch still another reign of terror. Very likely he fell victim to one of history's shrewdest assassinations.

It takes a shrewd eye and ample political skill to be a successful pirate. Tragically, the route is clogged with brutes and boneheads who leave a swath of damage and destruction behind them. They often get their just deserts, like the movie villains we love to hate. Our advice is to consider a different route. You and those around you will probably all be better off. But if you're sure it's your calling—or your karma—check out some of the references provided at the end of the chapter. In addition to watching over their shoulders and covering their backsides, travelers on mugger's lane need as much guidance as they can muster.

FRANK 'N' HOPE: *THE WAY OF THE PIRATE*

Frank:	Let me guess. You think we should all be into service. Love your neighbor and your customer and all that baloney.
Hope:	You've got a better idea?
Frank:	Piracy sounds pretty good to me. Adventure! Treasure!
Hope:	A lot of pirates got hanged. But how much adventure and treasure have you been finding?
Frank:	Are you kidding? No way in a job like mine.
Hope:	Your ship can't get out of port? Sounds more like bog than piracy.
Frank:	You should know.

THE PATH OF SERVICE: COURAGE AND GIVING

One path remains: highly fulfilling, but less often traveled. It's not an easy route to find or follow. Yet all the world's great spiritual traditions endorse the journey using similar terms—the path of faith and love in Judaism and Christianity, the peace of surrender to God in Islam, the Buddhist Eight-Fold Way, the yogas of Hinduism, the Tao of Lao Tzu. Across traditions, the spiritual journey spawns some of the world's most oft-told tales. These tales anchor the ennobling legends of all cultures.

Many authors have noted shared and timeless elements

or themes across different legends, myths, and heroic tales.* Consider a famous example, the life of Joan of Arc:

> A girl named Joan was born in 1412 to a family of tenant farmers in a small country town, Domrémy, in France. As a teenager, Joan began to hear voices calling her to lead France against English invaders. Certain that her calling came from God, she traveled to the castle occupied by the dauphin Charles, uncrowned heir to the throne of France. She told him it was her mission to defeat the British and enable him to be crowned at Reims, the cathedral city where French kings had been coronated since the fifth century. Charles and his counselors were initially skeptical, but Joan's piety, courage, and intelligence eventually prevailed. She led French forces to a series of dramatic victories against the English, and achieved her mission. Charles was coronated at Reims in 1429, with the 17-year-old Joan standing nearby. A year later, she was captured by the king's enemies and tried as a heretic. Despite relentless pressure to recant, she maintained to the end her faith that her voices had not deceived her. In May 1431, at the age of 19, she was burned at the stake. Her courage in the face of death led even some of the English to say, "We have burned a saint." A papal inquiry twenty-five years later annulled the

*The best-known discussion about the idea of a *monomyth,* a single narrative that cuts across time and place, is Joseph Campbell's *The Hero with a Thousand Faces* (Princeton, NJ: Princeton University Press, 1949). For a critical discussion of Campbell and of this literature, see chapters 15 and 16 in *The Spiritual Quest: Transcendence in Myth, Religion, and Science,* by Robert M. Torrance (Berkeley, CA: University of California Press, 1994).

> verdict, and after five centuries Joan was canonized by Pope Benedict XV. France celebrates four national holidays: Bastille Day, armistice days for both world wars, and May 2 in honor of St. Joan of Arc.

In Joan's life we see a pattern found repeatedly in human narratives both great and small. It appears in classic tales like *The Odyssey* and *Beowulf,* as well as popular narratives such as *Star Wars*, *The Lion King*, or *Titanic*. The stories typically begin with crisis or dislocation. Often, there is an ominous outside threat—a hostile army, a destructive beast, or a natural catastrophe. There is usually a demon within the spiritual traveler as well—doubt, indecision, or weakness. The crisis triggers a quest, a journey in search of resolution or transcendence. The hero or heroine leaves home, often because it is her calling and she has no choice. Joan left home to respond to God's call to defend her country against its enemies. Leaving home also casts away the shackles of routine and convention. The pressures and constraints of everyday life often keep us from seeing and fulfilling our potential. The quest is a time of great challenge and danger, when life and soul are in the balance. Joan faced a host of skeptics and enemies within the French elite, as well as earning the implacable hatred of the English.

The heroic victory is hard won and never certain. Joan overcame countless obstacles in leading French armies to remarkable victories, but was ultimately betrayed and martyred. Still, she clung to her faith and achieved Christlike transcendence in her death. But not all tales end in tragedy. The hero often succeeds after a noble struggle, and is prepared to return home, armed now with treasures or gifts. These sometimes include physical treasures like the Holy Grail. More often they are intangible symbols representing deeper psychic and spiritual treasures such as courage, power, wisdom, and faith.

Four gifts emerge repeatedly from the classic tales. The first is authorship: helping others to create their own composition, or paint their own canvas or invent something new. Giving authorship enables those around us to do something that they love doing, to use their chosen skills, and to express something important about their deeper selves. Think of a six-year-old who comes home from school clutching the three or four major works of art created that day and eagerly shares them with his parents. Too many workplaces drive out authorship by offering employees minimal discretion or room for self-expression. Instead, they reward them for following directions and adhering to procedures.

A second gift is power. In a world increasingly dominated by gigantic forces and institutions—the global economy, the spread of technology, big government, and giant multinationals—it's all too easy to feel dwarfed and helpless, at the mercy of forces over which we have no control. But feeling powerless is debilitating and corrosive. It often incites the dark side of human nature. All of us need to feel we can influence things we care about. You bequeath power when you help someone else to make a difference and to influence the world around them. Consider the traditional plight of production line workers. The words of one auto worker sum it up pretty well: "It's just like the army. No, it's worse than the army, 'cause you're welded to the line. You just about need a pass to piss." At Saturn and other progressive companies, the gift of power for production line workers comes in the form of a chain or cord to stop the line if they see a problem. As the manager of an auto plant in California put it, "We had heavy arguments about installing the cord here.

We wondered if workers would pull it just to get a rest. That has not happened."*

A third gift is love—individuals' caring and compassion for one another. Love is the basic glue that bonds families and societies together. Cynics ask what love has to do with anything at work. They can't understand how the two words belong in the same sentence. Their cynicism reveals a shallow and jaundiced understanding of both love and work. You give love when you take the risks of showing others genuine affection, caring, and appreciation. Love is largely absent in the modern workplace. "Most managers would never use the word in any context more profound than their feelings about food, films, or games. They shy away from love's deeper meanings, fearing both its power and its risks. Caring begins with knowing—it requires listening, understanding, and accepting."†

How often do you feel that anyone at work really knows you or cares about you? How often do you feel appreciated and recognized for who you are and what you contribute? For many of us the answer is rarely or never. A country song was titled "Take This Job and Shove It"—not love it. Yet one of the secrets of great groups and high-performing organizations turns out to be something very much like love. Warren Bennis says that the "genius of Great Groups is that they get remarkable people—strong individual achievers—to work together to get results. But these groups serve a second and equally important function: They provide psychic support and personal fellowship. They help generate courage. Without a sounding board for outrageous ideas,

*J. Holusha, "No Utopia, but to Workers, It's a Job," *The New York Times,* Jan. 29, 1989, section 3, p. 1.

†Lee G. Bolman and Terrence E. Deal, *Leading with Soul: An Uncommon Journey of Spirit* (San Francisco: Jossey-Bass, 1995), p. 104.

without personal encouragement and perspective when we hit a roadblock, we'd all lose our way."* Put another way, greatness is easier to achieve when you love your work and the people you do it with.

Listen to Herb Kelleher, the maverick CEO who helped make Southwest Airlines consistently the most profitable firm in its industry. He insists that love is at the heart of Southwest's success, and that his love for his 18,000 employees is returned in a "spontaneous, voluntary overflowing of emotion."† People talk a lot about love at Southwest: they fly out of Love Field in Dallas; their symbol on the New York Stock Exchange is LUV; the employee newsletter is called *Luv Lines*; and their twentieth anniversary slogan was "20 Years of Loving You." They hold an annual "Heroes of the Heart" ceremony to honor those who have gone above and beyond even Southwest's high standards of duty. Is it all just corporate smoke and mirrors? Employees don't seem to think so. As one of them put it, "Herb loves us. We love Herb. We love one another. We love the company. One of the primary beneficiaries of our collective caring is our passengers." That kind of compassionate enthusiasm works out pretty well for everyone. Southwest's costs are lower than its competitors' for the simple reason that its people love their work, have fun doing it, and manage to be a lot more productive than their counterparts at other airlines.

The fourth gift is significance, with its dual implications of importance and meaningfulness. You give significance by helping others find deep meaning and a higher calling in

*Warren Bennis and Patricia Ward Biederman, *Organizing Genius: The Secrets of Creative Collaboration* (New York: Perseus, 1998), p. 135.
†Charles Farkas and Philippe De Backer, *Maximum Leadership: The World's Leading CEOs Share Their Five Strategies for Success* (New York: Holt, 1996), p. 87.

work and life. To feel significant is to feel that you matter and that your work makes the world a richer place. When we say that our job is nothing more than a paycheck, or that we'd quit in a minute if we could, we're saying that our work is meaningless, stunting life rather than enhancing it. The point is made in a very old story about an interviewer who talked to three stonemasons about their work:

> INTERVIEWER (to first stonemason): What are you doing?
> FIRST STONEMASON: (Growling) What's it look like I'm doing? Are you blind? I'm cutting stone!
> INTERVIEWER (to second stonemason): What are you doing?
> SECOND STONEMASON: I'm cutting stone for the cathedral over there.
> INTERVIEWER (to third stonemason): And you, what are you doing?
> THIRD STONEMASON: I'm serving God.

It helps to work on a product or service you believe in. There's a big advantage to working in a place that builds an intimate connection between work and some greater good. It helps a lot if your workplace is committed to values and if it creates opportunities to explore and reinforce the significance of what you do. You need to find work that's right for you, and gives you a chance to make a difference. But as important as the work itself is the meaning you find in it.

These and other gifts earned on the spiritual journey have to come from the heart—they're gifts of self. But why give at all? Two reasons. One is the sheer pleasure and satisfaction in the act itself. The second is that things get pretty miserable in any group or organization when no one gives anything to anyone else. Hell is a family or workplace where everyone feels too wounded or self-important to care about others. Almost all of us know the pain. If you're stuck there, you know how bad it can get.

FRANK 'N' HOPE: *A NEW PATH*

Frank:	The smart money's still on the pirates.
Hope:	You've been saying that your whole life, Frank. What's it got you?
Frank:	It got me this far.
Hope:	A job you hate? A career that's going nowhere?
Frank:	You got a better idea?
Hope:	Frank, you're a chronic pain in the neck—but I like you anyway. I've got some ideas on how we could work together.
Frank:	Doing what?
Hope:	Oh . . . making this a better place to work. Getting our careers in gear. Having some fun.
Frank:	You serious?
Hope:	Very. Interested?
Frank:	Keep talking. I'm listening.

The high road of faith and service carries the blessings of all the world's religions, not to mention the endorsement of many contemporary gurus. But it's not an easy path. It entails risk and willingness to journey into the unknown. There will be dark valleys of despair as well as bright peaks of triumph. Your efforts to give and serve sometimes provoke suspicion or exploitation from others. You'll need all the courage and wisdom you can muster to meet the many challenges along the way. If you're lost in the fog, trapped in a bog, or bruised or paranoid from your travels along mugger's lane, now is a good time to think about a different direction. You won't run into Dilbert or Wally along the way, but their lives are in shambles. There's little evidence that Dilbert has ever had a successful date or a productive day at work. Even his dog regularly turns on him. He's been a huge success on the comic page, but who would want to trade places with him? There are much better options. Find the ones that are right for you.

ESCAPING CLUELESSNESS XII: CHOOSING A PATH

- WHICH PATH ARE YOU FOLLOWING?
  - FOG—YOU'RE NOT SURE WHERE YOU'RE HEADED.
  - BOG—YOU'RE TOO MIRED IN THE MUCK TO GET WHERE YOU WANT TO GO.
  - PIRACY—YOU'RE SEEKING ADVENTURE AND TREASURE, VIA PLUNDER IF NECESSARY.
  - SERVICE—IN SEARCH OF A BETTER LIFE AND BETTER WORLD.
- IF YOU'RE GOING NOWHERE, OR IN THE WRONG DIRECTION, FIND A BETTER PATH.

Looking Ahead

- We're in the early stages of two major movements:
  - —A global spiritual transition as humans around the globe struggle to make sense of life in a vastly changed world
  - —A gentle and constructive workplace revolution, fueled from below as well as from above by people who've made their own escape from cluelessness

SUGGESTIONS FOR FURTHER READING

Stephen Covey's classic, *The Seven Habits of Highly Successful People*, provides a highly readable introduction to prioritization, values, and time management. Jon Kabat-Zinn's *Wherever You Go, There You Are* is a readable and practical guide to meditation.

Helpful—and ecumenical—discussions of the spirituality of everyday life can be found in Father Paul Keenan's *Good News for Bad Days*, Rabbi Harold Kushner's *Who Needs God?* and Thomas Moore's *Care of the Soul.* Excellent books on work and spirit include Jim Autry's *Love and Profit*, Allen Briskin's *The Stirring of Soul in the Workplace*, David Whyte's *The Heart Aroused*, and (forgive our lack of humility) our own *Leading with Soul.*

If piracy is your destiny, head immediately to your nearest library or bookstore, where there's almost bound to be a copy of Niccolò Machiavelli's (almost) 500-year-old classic, *The Prince.* Although offensive to the ethically squeamish, the book offers a penetrating and powerful discussion of strategies for getting, keeping, and using power. Other provocative choices include Saul Alinsky's *Rules for Radicals*, John Kotter's *Power and Influence*, Michael Korda's *Power: What It Is and How to Get It*, and Ronna Lichtenberg's *Work Would Be Great if It Weren't for the People.*

See the Bibliography for publication details of these books.

Bibliography

Adams, Scott. *Build a Better Life by Stealing Office Supplies.* Kansas City, MO: Andrews and McMeel, 1991.

———. *Bring Me the Head of Willy the Mailboy.* Kansas City, MO: Andrews and McMeel, 1995.

———. *Dogbert's Top Secret Management Handbook.* New York: HarperBusiness, 1996.

———. *The Dilbert Principle.* New York: HarperBusiness, 1996.

———. *Seven Years of Highly Defective People.* Kansas City, MO: Andrews and McMeel, 1997.

———. *The Joy of Work: Dilbert's Guide to Finding Happiness at the Expense of Your Co-Workers.* New York: HarperBusiness, 1998.

Alinsky, Saul. *Rules for Radicals.* New York: Vintage Books, 1971.

Argyris, Chris. "Skilled Incompetence." *Harvard Business Review,* September 1986.

Autry, J. A. *Love and Profit.* New York: Avon, 1991.

Bennis, Warren. *Why Leaders Can't Lead: The Unconscious Conspiracy Continues.* San Francisco: Jossey-Bass, 1989.

Bennis, Warren, and Patricia Ward Biederman. *Organizing Genius: The Secrets of Creative Collaboration.* New York: Perseus, 1998.

Bolman, Lee G., and Terence E. Deal. *Leading with Soul: An Uncommon Journey of Spirit.* San Francisco: Jossey-Bass, 1995.

Briskin, A. *The Stirring of Soul in the Workplace.* San Francisco: Jossey-Bass, 1998.

Buchalter, G. "Finally, She Could Be Her Own Person." *Parade,* August 9, 1998.

Burrough, Bryan, and John Helyar. *Barbarians at the Gate.* New York: Harper, 1990.

Business Week. "Executive Pay," April 20, 1998; April 19, 1999.

Byrne, J. A. "How Al Dunlap Self-Destructed." *Business Week*, July 6, 1998.

Campbell, Joseph. *The Hero with a Thousand Faces*. Princeton, NJ: Princeton University Press, 1949.

Canedy, Dana. "Sunbeam's Board, in Revolt, Ousts Job-Cutting Chairman." *The New York Times*, June 16, 1998.

Caproni, Paula. "Work/Life Balance: You Can't Get There From Here." *Journal of Applied Behavioral Science*, 33(1), 1997.

Cleary, T. *The Essential Tao*. San Francisco: Harper, 1992.

Colvin, G. "The 50 Best Companies for Asians, Blacks and Hispanics." *Fortune*, July 19, 1999.

Covey, Stephen. *The Seven Habits of Highly Successful People*. New York: Fireside, 1990.

Deal, Terrence E., and Allan Kennedy. *Corporate Cultures*. Reading, MA: Addison-Wesley, 1982.

———. *The New Corporate Cultures*. Reading, MA: Perseus Books, 1999.

Deutsch, Claudia H. "Software That Can Make a Grown Company Cry." *The New York Times*, November 8, 1998.

Farkas, Charles M., and Phillippe De Backer. *Maximum Leadership: The World's Leading CEOs Share Their Five Strategies for Success*. New York: Holt, 1996.

Feinberg, M., and J. J. Tarrant. *Why Smart People Do Dumb Things*. New York: Simon & Schuster, 1995.

Fisher, Roger, and William Ury. *Getting to Yes*. Boston: Houghton Mifflin, 1981.

Friedman, T. L. "Big Mac II." *The New York Times*, December 11, 1996.

Hamilton, Denise. "Dog vs. Man: Two High-Powered Management Experts Go Paw to Hand Over Workplace Issues." *Los Angeles Times*, February 24, 1997.

Hillman, James. *The Soul's Code: In Search of Character and Calling*. New York: Random House, 1996.

Holusha, J. "No Utopia, but to Workers, It's a Job." *The New York Times*, January 29, 1989.

Holy Bible: New Revised Standard Version. Oxford: Oxford University Press, 1989.

Jackson, Phil. *Sacred Hoops: Spiritual Lessons of a Hardwood Warrior*. New York: Hyperion, 1995.

Kabat-Zinn, Jon. *Wherever You Go, There You Are: Mindfulness Meditation in Everyday Life*. New York: Hyperion, 1995.

Katzenbach, Jon R., and Douglas K. Smith. *The Wisdom of Teams: Creating the High Performance Organization*. Boston: Harvard Business School Press, 1993.

Keenan, Father Paul. *Good News for Bad Days: Living a Soulful Life*. New York: Warner, 1998.

Kotter, John. *Power and Influence: Beyond Formal Authority*. New York: Free Press, 1985.

Korda, Michael. *Power: What It Is and How to Get It*. Los Angeles: Warner, 1991.

Kushner, Rabbi Harold. *Who Needs God?* New York: Summit, 1989.

Lawler, Edward A. *From the Ground Up: Six Principles for Building the New Logic Corporation*. San Francisco: Jossey-Bass, 1996.

Lawrence, Paul, and Jay Lorsch. *Organization and Environment*. Boston: Harvard Business School, Division of Research, 1967.

Levering, R., and M. Moskowitz. *The 100 Best Companies to Work for in America*. New York: Plume, 1993.

Levine, Daniel S. *Disgruntled: The Darker Side of the World of Work*. New York: Berkley Boulevard Books, 1998.

L'Express. "Les circuits effarants de l'argent en Corse" ["The incredible money circuits in Corsica"], June 18, 1998.

Lichtenberg, Ronna. *Work Would Be Great if It Weren't for the People*. New York: Hyperion, 1998.

Lundin, William, and Kathleen Lundin. *When Smart People Work for Dumb Bosses: How to Survive in a Crazy and Dysfunctional Workplace*. New York: McGraw-Hill, 1998.

Lyall, S. "Shirkers Unite! Tomorrow Is Your Day." *The New York Times*, April 5, 1998.

Machiavelli, Niccolò. *The Prince*. New York: Bantam, 1984.

Mintzberg, Henry. *Structure in Fives: Designing Effective Organizations*. Englewood Cliffs, NJ: Prentice-Hall, 1993.

Moore, Thomas. *Care of the Soul: A Guide for Cultivating Depth and Sacredness in Everyday Life*. New York: HarperCollins, 1991.

Oshry, Barry. *Seeing Systems: Unlocking the Mysteries of Organizational Life*. San Francisco: Berrett-Koehler, 1995.

Peirce, E., C. A. Smolinski, and B. Rosen. "Why Sexual Harassment

Complaints Fall on Deaf Ears." *The Academy of Management Executives*, 12(3), August 1998.

Pfeffer, Jeffrey. *Competitive Advantage through People: Unleashing the Power of the Work Force*. Boston: Harvard Business School Press, 1994.

———. *Managing with Power: Politics and Influence in Organizations*. Boston: Harvard Business School Publishing, 1992.

———. "Six Dangerous Myths About Pay." *Harvard Business Review*, May-June, 1998.

Quinn, D. William, Monica Stewart, and Jeri Nowakowski. "An External Evaluation of Systemwide School Reform in Chicago." *International Journal of Education Reform*, January 1993.

Schein, Ed. *Organization Culture and Leadership*. San Francisco: Jossey-Bass, 1992.

Senge, Peter. *The Fifth Discipline: The Art and Practice of the Learning Organization*. New York: Doubleday/Currency, 1990.

———. *The Fifth Discipline Fieldbook: Strategies and Tools for Building a Learning Organization*. New York: Doubleday/Currency, 1994.

Serwer, Andy. "How Bill Gates Invests His Money." *Fortune*, March 15, 1999.

Solomon, Norman. *The Trouble with Dilbert: How Corporate Culture Gets the Last Laugh*. Monroe, ME: Common Courage Press, 1997.

Sobel, Robert. *When Giants Stumble: Classic Business Blunders and How to Avoid Them*. Paramus, NJ: Prentice-Hall, 1999.

Tillson, Tamsen. "Is Your Career Killing You?" *Canadian Business*, September 26, 1997.

Torrance, Robert M. *The Spiritual Quest: Transcendence in Myth, Religion, and Science*. Berkeley: University of California Press, 1994.

Weber, Max. *Wirtschaft und Gesellschaft, 1922*. First published in English as *The Theory of Economic and Social Organization*. Talcott Parsons, translator. New York: Free Press, 1947.

Whitaker, B. "If You Can't Dodge Dilbert, Hire Him." *The New York Times*, June 29, 1997.

Whyte, David. *The Heart Aroused*. New York: Currency Doubleday, 1994.

Index

About the Authors

Lee G. Bolman and Terrence E. Deal first met in 1976 when they opted to co-teach a course on organizations in the same Harvard University classroom. Trained in different disciplines on opposite coasts, they found little common ground. In their first joint course, they devoted significant lecture time to debunking each other's fallacies. As curious academics, Lee and Terry found their disagreements intellectually exciting. Few of their students agreed. Most were convinced that their instructors were either incompetent or deviously manipulative.

Rumors and stories about the strange events in Bolman and Deal's classroom spread through the school. Sarcastic asides crept into faculty meetings. A student delegation protested to the Dean, who called and politely inquired, "What's going on?" The odd couple responded with a claim of "academic freedom." The Dean seemed placated—for a while at least.

Few things are more unifying than a common enemy—in this case, a formidable combination of Lee's and Terry's students, colleagues, and boss. It was a powerful incentive to find a common scripture to accommodate their diverse perspectives.

The duo eventually achieved a blinding flash of the obvious. Individually, each brought important insights about organizations. Instead of being fundamentally incompatible, those different perspectives each provided important pieces to a larger puzzle. Out of this came their first book, *Modern Approaches to Understanding and Managing Organizations*. It argued that organizations were simultaneously factories, families, jungles, and theaters or temples. The idea that people view reality through different lenses led to the publication of *Reframing Organizations: Artistry, Choice, and Leadership*. There, Bolman and Deal argued that the ability to look at situations from multiple perspectives is crucial to leadership.

For five years, Bolman and Deal co-directed the National Center for Educational Leadership (NCEL), a research consortium of Harvard, Vanderbilt, and the University of Chicago. The center's mission was to identify and disseminate the ingredients of effective leadership to those struggling to shape America's schools. During this work, Bolman and Deal developed solid empirical evidence to support their earlier claim that the ability to use multiple frames increases leaders' and managers' ability to figure out what's really going on and what they can do about it. Their research showed that individuals who prefer to see the world as rational and results-oriented made good managers, but poor leaders. Leaders, on the other hand, emphasized symbols and meaning.

This distinction paved the way for the publication of *Leading with Soul: An Uncommon Journey of Spirit*. There, Bolman and Deal focused on the spiritual side of organizations, and argued that the heart of leadership lies in the hearts of leaders. Like their earlier books, *Leading with Soul* has been translated into multiple languages for readers around the world.

This odd couple has come a long way. Although their

careers have taken them to different locations, they are still joined at the hip.

Lee G. Bolman is an author, scholar, consultant and lecturer, who currently holds the Marion Bloch Missouri Chair in Leadership at the University of Missouri–Kansas City.

He has written numerous books on leadership and organizations with co-author Terry Deal, including *Leading with Soul: An Uncommon Journey of Spirit, Reframing Organizations: Artistry, Choice, and Leadership, The Path to School Leadership, Becoming a Teacher Leader,* and *Modern Approaches to Understanding and Managing Organizations.* Bolman's and Deal's books have been translated into more than ten languages.

Bolman consults and lectures worldwide to corporations, public agencies, universities, and schools. He holds a B.A. in History and a Ph.D. in Organizational Behavior from Yale University. Prior to assuming his current position, he taught for more than twenty years at Harvard University.

He lives in Kansas City, Missouri, with his wife, Joan Gallos, the two youngest of his six children, Christopher and Bradley, and an orthopedically challenged Dalmatian, Vincent Van Gogh of KCMO.

Terrence E. Deal is an author, teacher, and consultant, and the Irving R. Melbo Professor of Education at USC's Rossier School. He previously taught at Harvard, Stanford, and Vanderbilt Universities.

Deal's consulting spans across all sectors: business, education, health care, and military organizations. His travels take him to Europe, Asia, the Middle East, and South America. He has written twenty books and more than 100 articles and book chapters concerning organizations, leadership, change, culture, symbolism, and spirit. His most recent book is *The New Corporate Cultures: Revitalizing the Workplace after Downsizing, Merger, and Reengineering.*

Deal holds a B.A. in History from the University of LaVerne, an M.A. in Educational Administration from California State University at Los Angeles, and a Ph.D. in Education and Sociology from Stanford University.

He lives in San Luis Obispo, California, with his wife Sandy and a cat named Max.